CAREERS IN
SOCIAL WORK

CAREERS IN SOCIAL WORK

By

Carolyn Simpson and
Dwain Simpson

THE ROSEN PUBLISHING GROUP, INC.
New York

Published in 1992 by The Rosen Publishing Group, Inc.
29 East 21st Street, New York, NY 10010

First Edition

Simpson, Carolyn.
    Careers in social work / by Carolyn Simpson and Dwain Simpson.
— 1st ed.
        p.   cm.
    Includes bibliographical references and index.
    Summary: A discussion of the career opportunities in social work, how to get involved, where to get more information, and how to prepare for a career in this area.
    ISBN 0-8239-1407-0
    1. Social service—Vocational guidance—United States—Juvenile literature. [1. Social service—Vocational guidance. 2. Vocational guidance.] I.Simpson, Dwain, 1951-   . II. Title.
HV10.5.S56   1992
361.3'2'02373—dc20   91-14457
                                                                            CIP
                                                                            AC

Manufactured in the United States of America

About the Authors

Carolyn Simpson has worked as a social worker for ten years, first as a Human Services intern, then as a clinical social worker (in both an inpatient and an outpatient setting), and finally as a school counselor. She holds a Bachelor's degree in Sociology from Colby College, Waterville, Maine, and a Master's degree in Human Relations from the University of Oklahoma. She has taught classes in the social sciences at Oscar Rose Junior College, Midwest City, Oklahoma, and in an alternative high school in Bridgton, Maine.

Dwain Simpson is a Licensed Clinical Social Worker at Laureate Psychiatric Clinic and Hospital in Tulsa, Oklahoma. He holds a Bachelor's degree in Political Science and a Master's in Social Work from the University of Oklahoma. For the past thirteen years he has worked as a clinical social worker in community agencies in both Oklahoma and Maine, and he maintained a private practice in Portland, Maine, for six of those years.

The Simpsons are the authors of another book by The Rosen Publishing Group: *Coping with Emotional Disorders*. They live on the outskirts of Tulsa with their three children—plus a dog, a cat, and a rabbit.

Contents

Preface

If you're like me at your age, you don't really consider career opportunities until your teacher assigns you the task. Back in sixth grade the kids in my class were supposed to research several professions and then choose the one we wanted to make our life's work. Our teacher didn't tell us what factors we should consider in selecting a profession. Would it be job satisfaction (whatever that was), money, or prestige, and did any of those go together? Most of my classmates went for the money—and if they had followed their plans the world would now be saturated with doctors and lawyers from my sixth-grade class.

I, on the other hand, looked into social work because I thought the job sounded interesting, and if there was one thing I had already decided I wanted to avoid, it was a boring job. My friends laughed at my choice. "Isn't that just like a girl?" they said, or words to that effect. "Wanting to help people."

What they didn't know is that social workers *can* in certain situations make a lot of money—and hold powerful positions in the community. Social workers are no longer those people who doled out monthly welfare checks and then followed clients around to see how they were spending the money. Increasingly, social workers are finding their way into businesses, community organizations, and the therapy room.

Research has also discovered that the two most versatile

degrees in our society today are the MBA and the MSW. Social workers, by virtue of their training in group work, their knowledge of community resources, and their independence and initiative, can use their talents in a widening variety of settings. You may discover as you get older that you hate the idea of spending the next forty years in the same profession. Social work is a field in which you can switch jobs without having to return to college for additional degrees.

In this book Dwain and I attempt to give you some history of social work, an overview of the career opportunities in the field, and the qualities a person working in it should possess. To assist you in your career planning, we have also included a chapter on how to select a college and how to make the best of your high school education.

Naturally, money is important in choosing a career. People can't pay the rent and buy groceries from "good deeds" alone. Nonetheless, there is much to be said for liking what you do, feeling that you are making a worthwhile contribution in your work, and playing a role in social change.

Many social workers have given freely of their time and ideas to make this book complete. For their help, we are grateful to Helen Boyd, Shaun Kieran, Deborah Winner Burns, Sallie Clote, Wayne Chess, Nancy Chess, Chene Tucker, Marla Harris, Nelda Spyres, Lenore Johnson, Georgia Ann Gibson, Rich O'Toole, Gary Mitchell, Diane Hays, Mary Miller, and Leah Hunt.

Many thanks, too, to all those who graciously let us portray them in our pages here.

Part 1

Understanding Social Work

Chapter I

A History of Social Work

Throughout the ages people have donned the cap of social worker—helping their neighbor in time of need. But in the beginning social work was not a bona fide profession. Social workers were simply people in the community who did "good deeds." And they were not paid for them. Two significant events changed all that: the Industrial Revolution and urbanization. When the United States started to change from an agricultural country into a modern industrial nation, people flocked to the cities, abandoning the farms for jobs. Immigrants poured in from their homelands, and there in rundown city tenements they found themselves. People who in the past had needed huge families to work the farms found themselves saddled with too many mouths to feed.

Subsequent poverty, unemployment, and an increasing number of immigrants who did not understand the ways of urban society led to greater social disorganization. In the past the mentally ill person, the pauper, and the criminal were all handled in the community. In the anonymity of the cities, state government groups arose to deal with them. Other watchdog groups followed to see that the socially disadvantaged were treated appropriately.

Thus two sets of people sprang up out of the circumstances—one set who wanted to find ways to help the needy, and another set who theorized about the causes (and solutions) of those new problems. The two groups, with their conflicting views of "the problem," joined together to form the American Social Science Association (ASSA) in 1865. Still, these people could not agree on the appropriate focus for their work—should they work to change the causes of the problems or should they concentrate on treating persons beset by poverty, poor sanitation, and joblessness? One group became the workers, the other remained tied to their theories—trying to pinpoint environmental causes of poverty with a view to reform. The "doers" and the "thinkers" could not get along. Finally, in 1874, the work segment of the group withdrew and formed the Conference of Charities, which later became the National Conference of Charities and Corrections (NCCC).

Two people who lent support to the social work movement (although they were not officially social workers since the term had yet not been coined, nor the profession created) were Dorothea Dix and Jane Addams. Dorothea Dix began her work in the mid-1800s, volunteering to teach Sunday School for prison inmates. What she discovered in 1841 was that the mentally ill prisoners were housed alongside the criminals, with no provision made for treating their illnesses. Dorothea Dix spent the rest of her life lobbying for improved prison conditions for the mentally ill.

Jane Addams (who was not even born when Dorothea Dix started working for prison reform) was concerned with the poor people, especially the children, who lived in the slums of the cities. She knew that their housing was inadequate, that play space was nonexistent, and that the residents resorted to burglary and delinquency because there was not enough food to go around nor enough jobs to keep the adults fruitfully occupied.

Initially people had viewed the "afflicted" person as someone who was "morally weak" and so had brought on all present catastrophes, including sickness, unemployment, and poverty. The prevailing attitude of, "You get what you deserve" derived from the Puritan work ethic. Good people worked hard; lazy people didn't, and that supposedly explained the appalling conditions of poverty intermixed with the affluence of other neighborhoods.

The charity services that sprang up about this time—in the 1880s—were often run by well-to-do, educated young women who felt good about "doing something for the needy." Affluent community members gave freely as well, in part because they saw their giving of alms as a way to "enter the Kingdom of Heaven." They looked down on the people they helped. They saw themselves as superior because they had the money and position in the community not to need assistance.

The people who set up the first settlement houses had a different philosophy. They believed that what truly helped people of misfortune was "good neighboring." Giving charity to people only embarrassed them; what really helped was giving them *knowledge*—the means by which they could eventually help themselves. In settlement houses the "social workers" moved into the community lock, stock, and barrel. Once the people realized that the person was "one of them," they were receptive to the help offered.

Jane Addams lived a privileged life until she decided, after graduating from college, to pursue a lifelong goal of helping others in the city slums. She purchased a mansion on the longest straight road in the world—in Chicago—and settled in with some colleagues. At first she had only a vague idea of how she would help the neighbors. She did not want to patronize them. The neighbors, however, ended up telling her what they needed most. The day after they moved in a young mother appeared on the doorstep, two little children huddled beside her. The mother asked if Jane and her colleagues would watch her children for a while because the sitter had not come that day, and the mother couldn't risk being late to work. Jane Addams welcomed the children and even invited the mother to breakfast. Within a matter of days other neighbors brought their children, too, and Jane's Hull mansion (now called Hull House) offered its first service—day care. Jane Addams was remarkably gifted in attracting people with the skills she needed to help out at Hull House. Soon a kindergarten teacher was hired to run the day-care class for the children left in their care.

From day care, Jane Addams branched out into social clubs (a popular idea among settlement houses adopted from the English), because she found she could reach more people not by preaching to them, but by giving them a place to meet and exchange ideas. Because of the huge immigrant population, she encouraged the sharing of cultures so that the neighborhood children could feel proud of their parents and build on their identities, despite all the changes their families faced in this new country. The social clubs also presented the "American way of life" in a less threatening way. The residents learned how to cook nutritious meals and how to read and speak English. And because of the exchange of ideas, they were able to give back something of themselves. The settlement houses allowed—in fact encouraged—the neighbors *to give back to others.* "Giving back" kept them from feeling inferior and in need of charity.

Jane Addams's Hull House enjoyed a long history. Because of her "good neighboring," settlement houses sprang up in other cities such as Boston and New York. Jane Addams brought about the first public park for children in Chicago, improved the sanitation of the city, and encouraged the residents to take pride in their dwellings. She lobbied for safer working conditions and better schools. But more than that, she helped raise the self-esteem of the immigrants by valuing each person's past and helping that person fit into the present. In recognition of her lifelong achievements, Jane Addams received the Nobel Peace Prize in 1931, the first American woman to win the honor.

Settlement houses played an important role in social reform until after World War I, when the movement lost its momentum. Workers in these settlement houses joined the National Conference on Social Welfare (of which Jane Addams was the first woman president), and they began to think of themselves as a professional group—social workers.

At the same time the charity organizations were developing.

The charity organizations believed in giving to the poor and needy, but to do so properly they wanted to come up with ways to document the need for their services. That meant visiting the homes, witnessing the client's need, and then returning to the office to record what service was needed. Seeking to soften their stance somewhat by being "neighborly," too, they called these people "friendly visitors." Unfortunately, helpful as they were, they focused only on solving the person's problems one at a time and made no effort to change the conditions that might have led to the predicament.

Friendly visitors were at first volunteers: again, young, well-educated females. Men had more important jobs to do and money to be earned. Gradually, as the volunteers were replaced by paid workers, the "social workers" saw a need to connect themselves to a college to lend some professionalism to their ranks. In 1898 the charity organizations created the first school of philanthropy, which eventually became Columbia University School of Social Work. Some newly developed schools of social work emphasized apprenticeship programs so that the workers could put into practice what they learned in classes. Other schools wanted more emphasis on theory and academics so that the world would view social workers as professionals. (Until then the average citizen couldn't be sure just what social workers did—or were licensed to do.) Having an advanced degree in social work suggested that this was now a bona fide profession.

Social work focused on three major areas. The casework method focused on services for the individual (but some said it neglected the interplay of environmental factors). The second area—group work—arose from the social clubs of the settlement era and proved useful in restructuring community life. The American Association of Group Workers was created in 1946 and incorporated into the National Association of Social Workers (NASW) in 1956.

The third area of focus was organizational social work, as social workers looked toward implementing, coordinating, and changing existing services in agencies as a whole.

Relatively speaking, social work is a new profession, still working to define itself as late as the 1960s and 1970s. Social workers continue to struggle with their identity. In the recent past, people from other academic disciplines such as sociology, psychology, or education could "wear the social worker's hat," and there was no real way to monitor the profession. Now that NASW is defining who can call themselves social workers (and only those who have earned a specific degree in social work such as the BSW, MSW, or DSW can do so), more and more people are in agreement about the focus of treatment—not just the individual, but his whole *system*: his family interaction, his environment.

Social workers occupy a variety of positions in the community. They work in hospitals helping people link up with the resources they need when they are discharged. They work in private business, either assisting employers and employees in settling work-related disputes, or organizing new programs to assist management. They work in psychiatric settings much as psychologists work, and some have built prestigious careers from their workshops and writings. (Virginia Satir immediately comes to mind.) Some social workers assume supervisory roles; some work with prison inmates; some arrange adoptions and foster home placements. Some counsel young adults on reproductive issues; some work in the schools to intervene with troubled students. Some social workers teach other social workers, and if they teach in major universities they have the potential to make six-figure salaries. Other social workers choose to fight the system, to make lasting changes in the environment, and although they are not paid much to do that, they get tremendous satisfaction. Social workers are in the military and the Peace Corps, in recreation groups for children and in hospices for the terminally ill.

Chapter II

Qualities Needed for Social Work

Before we consider what qualities you need for social work, let's look at *why* people want to go into social work in the first place. I have already told you it is not a money-making profession. At best, you will make a satisfactory living (although some social workers do make an excellent living from private practice and college teaching). If you don't go into social work for the money, why *do* you go into it? Obviously you must have some compelling reason to do work that is sometimes dangerous, often stressful, and not well rewarded.

Before we go any further, let me tell you something about helping people. Needy people do not like needing help. Most people do not appreciate handouts; they feel at a disadvantage. The social worker's job, then, is to lend a helping hand without increasing the dependence of the recipient at the same time. Sometimes you have to take a good, hard look at *your* motives before you can be of any real help to people. You do not go into social work to feel better about your station in life. You have to feel some connection to these other people, and you have to believe that they have something to teach you, too.

If you asked a random group of people in the helping professions why they selected this type of work—and if they responded honestly—you would probably find that more than 50 percent wanted to learn more about *themselves*.

By studying the human mind, by helping others face

adversity, you learn things that you yourself can use. Nothing is wrong with entering the profession to help heal your own problems as long as you remember that to be effective you must be healthier than the client, and you can't rely on *him* or *her* to help you.

Many people will tell you that they have gone into the profession because it is gratifying work. Why is it gratifying? Is it because they think other people need them? Is it because they happen to have skills that are good in the work?

Some people are not certain *why* they went into this work. Dwain became interested in clinical social work after being assigned to a psychiatric hospital in his first-year field placement. Until then he had not been sure what he wanted to do.

I first considered social work after I learned that the education field was overflowing with elementary school teachers.

A friend (who is a psychologist now) could not decide in college whether to pursue psychology or drama. She took courses in both, unable to make up her mind. Finally she sought out one of her favorite teachers after class and asked him to help her make up her mind. She told him she was equally interested in both fields.

"What should I do?" she asked. She expected a lecture, a plan.

"The professor reached into his pocket and pulled out a coin. Without explaining further, he shoved the coin across the desk to her and said, "Flip it."

"What for?" my friend asked.

"Heads, you go into drama. Tails, you go on in psychology."

"You're kidding," she said. "That's it? That's your plan?"

She looked at the coin and then back at him. "But what if it comes up drama?" she asked, and it wasn't until that moment that she knew there was really only one choice.

People in the helping professions who are the most effective choose to help people because they are *good at it*. Pure and simple. You get satisfaction from doing what you do well.

So let's look at the qualities possessed by people who are

most effective in the helping professions—qualities that would be useful to possess even as a student.

Because your work brings you into contact with people every day, you need the ability to get along. More than just getting along, you need to *like* people, because needy people can sense insincerity a mile away. Chances are if you like someone you'll want to help him or her grow, not become dependent on the services you offer.

Working well with people means that you have good social skills. If you do not know how to conduct yourself in public, you had better take your cues from someone who does. Your image is important, and whether you choose to be or not, you will be a role model for many clients. Often you teach a client through example, not by giving specific advice. (If maturity and good manners are not your strong points, don't despair. I offer you a crash course in job skills and social skills in the last chapter.)

It is not enough simply to be gregarious; you also must be able to handle angry people—people who may not want your help in the first place. First learn to handle your own feelings—particularly anger—because you must be calm and reasonable when others are not. If you are ruled by your emotions, you will be as unpredictable as the people you are supposed to be helping. Anger is energizing—it's not all bad—so it is important to use it as long as you can channel it into constructive activities.

Social workers have been called diplomats at times. You learn early on that there are times to take a stand and times to stand back. You may already possess those skills. Are you good at settling disputes between your friends? Do people look to you for a fair assessment of their problems?

Initiative is another quality you need, because in some jobs you will find yourself given little direction and great leeway. You may be the only social worker in the department, and it will be up to you to finish your paperwork on time, manage your caseload, and respond to crises as they occur. If you need someone telling you what to do every minute of the day, this will be a hard job for you. You must be the type of person who can decide just what needs to be done that day or down the line. Part of initiative is *anticipating* need, and that means thinking ahead and being prepared. Think about it. Are you the type of person who needs a lot of direction to finish a school project, or can you work independently?

Anyone with initiative may also be compulsive. The more polite term is organized, and if organization is not your strong suit either, don't worry. That is an area you can improve on, and I'll show you ways in the next chapter.

When I started working as a social worker in a private psychiatric hospital, I was overwhelmed the first day with paperwork, a heavy caseload, and a list of rules a mile long. The other two workers were psychologists, and although they had already been there a few weeks they were just as over-whelmed. At the end of the first week when I turned in my paperwork on time, my boss praised me and my colleagues groaned. They were still a week behind. Later I took them aside and apologized for making them feel less competent. "It's just that I'm a compulsive person," I said. "Social work has taught me to organize my time and to make peace with paperwork."

If you are to work independently, you must learn to organize your time and to establish priorities. Otherwise you'll be star-ing at a mountain of paperwork and coming in evenings to catch up.

A friend of ours is a medical social worker and also the director of her department. She may go for weeks at a time without seeing another social worker because they are all as-signed to separate wings of the hospital. Sallie cannot schedule her day because she covers the emergency room, and everyone knows that it is subject to the whims of accident. So Sallie demonstrates another trait of the successful social worker: independence. Independence and initiative go hand in hand. You have to be independent (and autonomous) to handle the isolation that you may feel from other social workers. And you need initiative to know what to do with your time when you spend so much of it without guidance.

When I started as a psychiatric social worker in a hospital in

Maine, the clinical director gave me a brief orientation to their services and the paperwork. That instruction lasted two hours on a Saturday morning. When I arrived on Monday no one greeted me at the door. Instead, word had been left at the front desk for me to come up to the floor and *begin work*. I remember walking into the nurse's station and saying, "I'm here."

A nurse pointed to names in blue chalk on the blackboard. "Those are your patients," she said.

"That's it?" I asked. "What you do want me to do?"

"Whatever it is that social workers do," the nurse answered.

Fortunately, I had been around hospitals long enough to know what I was supposed to do. The inexperienced social worker might be in for a shock.

It is not enough to be independent and self-starting; you also must be resourceful. That does not mean very clever or a walking encyclopedia of resources. It simply means you must know where to look for help, because most of the time you will be the one responsible for finding that help.

People learn early to be resourceful. Are you able to find a store that sells a vintage rookie baseball card when all your friends swear it doesn't exist? Are you enough of a quick thinker that when your parents say, "If you earn $500 we'll foot the rest of the cost for a car," you can come up with the money (legitimately) within a couple of months? That's resourcefulness.

Successful social workers can carry on conversations with people all the while stockpiling information for future resources. If you have to help a homeless person find transportation back to Iowa, it helps to know a few organizations that have funds for that kind of thing. If you meet with a family who can no longer look after Aunt Eunice because they work during the day and she has started wandering the streets looking for them, it helps to know what to do with Aunt Eunice during the day.

If you are dependent on writing grants to fund your latest project (as community organizers do), you have to be resourceful at *finding* the money when the economy is tight. If you work in a business setting, you have to be both diplomatic and resourceful to smooth over labor disputes. Diplomatic, because touchy situations call for finesse; resourceful, because often the solutions are not waiting around to be discovered.

The next quality you need is harder to describe. It is the ability to recognize and maintain boundaries. The good social worker knows, particularly in a therapy setting, that those she helps will become dependent on her at some point. She cannot encourage that dependence because *true helping* is allowing clients to help themselves. Otherwise you strip people of their dignity. That is easier said than done. Sometimes you are tempted to let a client hang onto your coattails because it feels good to be needed and admired. You have to be able to let go of your clients when they are ready to go.

You also must be able to stay separate from the client's problems, or you will find yourself sinking into despair too. When you work with a client you cannot confuse the situation by playing racquetball with him after sessions. You do not enter into deals with clients, and you do not date them, no matter how attractive they are and how close they are to terminating services. When you enter into an arrangement to help someone, you make an unwritten deal to focus on *his* or *her* problems. You owe it to the client to leave your own troubles and expectations out of it. If you tend to wind up depressed because you overidentify with your clients and their problems, it will take a lot of energy to maintain your boundaries in this work. Having a strong sense of self helps to avoid losing yourself in other people's problems.

Whatever your particular prejudices are, if you cannot keep them out of your encounters with the people you help, you will not be helping them at all. That is not to say that you must not have any convictions. It merely means that you must not foist *your* values onto the client. It does not help to call a person stupid or lazy for not having secured a job. Judging someone harshly only alienates both of you. If you categorize people before getting to know them, you are too judgmental to be working with them in this fashion. You support people by valuing their humanity, not by whether they live up to your expectations. Listen more than you speak; that way your mouth won't get you in trouble.

Speaking of listening, the good social worker listens with heart as well as ears. To treat a client with respect, you have to value what he or she says and how *he* or *she* defines the problem. You cannot listen to a few words and then take over the story. You keep listening until he or she has finished talking, and even then you try to hear what is not being said. A good listener is not quick to jump to conclusions.

Are you someone to whom other kids confide their problems? If so, it is probably because you are a good listener and can keep your mouth shut afterward. If you are *not* a good listener, it is another trait you can cultivate. Practice really listening to others. Don't prepare your response while they are still talking. Having a ready reply makes it seem as though you had stopped listening halfway through their talking. Let them finish, and if necessary repeat the gist of what they said to be sure you understood it.

Are you good at keeping secrets? In social work there are always secrets to be kept. Confidentiality demands that you not discuss your caseload with others, that you not report names to other agencies (except in the case of abuse), and that you do not joke about clients with your secretary. (Good sense also dictates all the above.) You can't titillate your roommate with, "Guess who came into the mental health center today?" or "Guess how much the Thompsons make a year?" On the other hand, if you uncover child abuse you are obligated by law to report it. Some secrets are not meant to be kept.

You need to have empathy for a person you help, and if you don't have it to begin with, I can't tell you how to get it. You can't learn it in school; you can't order it from a catalog. Empathy is not the same as sympathy, which is misconstrued as pity. *People in need do not want pity*. Employees coming to you to settle a dispute do not want you to feel sorry for them. They want you to understand how the situation feels to them so that you can do something about it. Empathy is stepping into the other person's shoes for the moment. If you cannot imagine how it feels to a woman to have to send her children to bed hungry because she does not have enough money to buy food, you cannot help her because you simply do not understand. Empathy is understanding another person's predicament without necessarily *liking* the person or condoning how she got into the predicament.

Of course, you must not go to the other extreme, getting so bogged down worrying about this mother that you can't sleep at night. You will not be helpful then either, because you will be expending too much energy carrying *her* burdens. Empathy is the ability to see through another person's eyes; perspective allows you to step back and remember that you are *not* that person, but someone in a position to help him or her.

Successful social workers are assertive without being aggressive. If you are to advocate for other people, you have to stand up for them. That does not mean being haughty or demanding. It means standing up for what you believe even when it is scary to do so. Fortunately, even if you are shy, assertiveness is a trait you can learn. Often it comes from experience and self-confidence. Otherwise you can enroll in special assertiveness training groups.

To be an effective social worker you must have handled (or be handling) *your* personal problems. You cannot allow your own troubles to creep into your sessions with clients. You cannot allow your problem with authority figures to affect your discussions with your boss. You will accomplish nothing by treating him or her like the parent (or whoever) that threatens you. Social workers are human beings, and we all have our own idiosyncrasies and problems. We need to take care of our problem first, because people who come to us for help are looking for guidance in their own problems.

If you have read this far you may have noticed that I have not mentioned needing to be an honor roll student to become a social worker. Not all intelligent people get good grades. Some have a sixth sense about people and the way to help them. You don't get grades for intuition. Besides, you can always improve your grades, but you cannot readily develop that knack for understanding people. Sensitivity and common sense are far more valuable than book knowledge. (Nonetheless, I will show you ways to make the best of your high school years if getting good grades is a problem for you. You do have to get into college to specialize in social work.)

If you are not at the top of your class academically, it's still okay. You will have to read a lot, however, because effective social workers must keep abreast of current theories and research findings in their area of specialization. If you are not an avid reader, cultivate the habit now.

Notice, too, that I have not said your odds of getting a job are enhanced by being a male or a female. The sad thing is that the lower-paying social work positions are usually occupied by women. The more prestigious, higher-paying positions are held by men, or evenly divided with women. Women first dominated the profession because it did not pay well and was considered by many to be a supplementary form of income. Women whose husbands had high-paying jobs could live comfortably on it; men who were a family's sole source of support could not.

If money is your greatest concern, this is probably not the field for you. You can make a good living as a social worker, but you have to enter the private sector for the big bucks.

If you have all the above qualities or most of them, you may think yourself a sterling individual. And you probably are, but that does not mean you would be able to do all people-oriented jobs well. For example, you would not do well in employment counseling jobs (in which you earn a commission by matching clients with jobs). If you have the "social worker" mentality, you would become overinvolved with the clients, taking on their other problems.

A similar problem happens in sales. As a salesman your objective is to sell as much as possible. If you are sidetracked by people's problems, you do not make the necessary sales. If you're more concerned with "bettering mankind" you will not necessarily be a good salesman.

Human resources departments in major businesses formerly

used social workers to mediate disputes. Nowadays they are seeking people who have specific degrees in Human Resources. Companies have found that social workers cannot always separate the work-related problem from the client's other problems. What starts out as a request to aid management turns into an ongoing session with the employee. "Social workers get too involved," these companies say.

Problems exist in social work as in every other profession. They are explained in detail in the chapters on specific jobs in Part 2. The greatest danger in the helping professions—whether it be psychology or social work or teaching—is *burnout*. It is hard to give of yourself, make yourself vulnerable, day in and day out and get little back. After a while (and the time involved depends on the stress of the job and the personality of the helper), you don't get enough job satisfaction to go on. Social work generally is not a profession in which you can see instant results from your work. When someone breaks a leg, the doctor sets the bone. When the bone has healed the cast comes off, and the doctor knows he has done his job. It is not so simple for the social worker. In Human Services you may initially help a family get welfare assistance, but their problems have not ended. Follow-ups and more help are needed. Therapy clients are not necessarily "cured" in one session. In fact, you will not necessarily "cure" them in any number of sessions. All this repetitive work, coupled with low pay, can lead to burnout.

But by the same token, words cannot convey the satisfaction of having successfully intervened in someone's life. It is a good feeling to know that you have made a difference. And although the work can be grueling, it is rarely dull because people are rarely dull. Only the paperwork is tedious, and you will find that the case in every profession.

Chapter III

Educational Requirements and Preparation

In this chapter we shall discuss the best way to prepare for the social work profession. First let's discuss the several social work degrees, the merits of each, and the drawbacks of degrees in a related field.

Many people get their first job when they have completed their BSW (Bachelor of Social Work) degree. Not all colleges offer that degree, however, so check into the program's availability when you select your college. With a BSW you can enter *some* social work jobs, but nowadays employers are demanding the MSW (Master of Social Work) as a prerequisite.

The BSW is granted after completion of four years of college and the required number of hours specializing in social work. Even at the undergraduate level, you are expected to do a field placement (working as a social worker intern) in a community agency, supervised by both your social work instructor and a supervisor in the agency. Nonetheless, the jobs you can pursue with only a BSW are limited. To be a therapist (a clinical social worker) or to work in a business setting, you need an MSW. This degree is a two-year, 60-credit-hour program beyond the bachelor's degree. Although MSW programs vary in curricula, as a rule you will be required to take courses in five areas: theories of human behavior, social policy, research, social work practice, and a practicum. During the first year you will spend a couple of days a week working at an agency (or with some other social work group) to integrate what you are learning with what goes on in the real world. In the second year the last semester may be devoted entirely to your field placement, or practicum. Between the first and second year of coursework you may be required to pass an examination. Failure may preclude you from continuing until you pass the section of the test you failed.

Beyond the MSW and BSW are the DSW (Doctor of Social Work) and the PhD in Social Work. With the current emphasis on specialization and longer years of schooling, these degrees may become more popular. At the moment, however, doctoral degrees are needed more for teaching than anything else.

Schools are now offering other social work degrees, such as the Bachelor of Arts in Social Work and the Master of Arts in Social Work. These degrees should not differ in course emphasis, but employers who are used to the BSW and MSW may not give the holders of these other degrees the same status. You will need to check in your state whether the BAs and MAs are considered the equivalent of the BSW and MSW degrees.

If you are serious about going into social work, go as far in your education as you can afford. Do not make the mistake I did. When I returned to graduate school, I couldn't decide between two master's programs—one in the Psychology department (Human Relations) and the other specifically in Social Work. Since my goal was to work as a Psychiatric Social Worker, I assumed either degree would be applicable. I finally chose the Human Relations degree for practical reasons: I could work on it at night while holding down a job during the day. With the social work program, I would have to take classes and do field placement during the day. To manage I would have to change to a night job, and I didn't think I could handle that and school, too.

So, trying to make the best of both worlds, I took social work classes in addition to my Human Relations work, but I specialized in marriage and family counseling within my own program. Now, you would have thought that in the long run I was better prepared to go into counseling than someone who had not had courses in counseling and theory. I learned—too late—that the social work profession was beginning to recognize only those who had specialized in that program. I could do the work—counseling families—but I was not eligible to call myself a social worker; I was a social work assistant.

In the future, if the NASW is successful, only those with a specific degree in social work will be able to hold down traditional social work jobs. By the time you finish college, social work assistants will probably be a thing of the past. Social work professors and members of the NASW believe (and I do not dispute it) that only those who have been steeped in the social work philosophy, theory, and systems approach can perform as social workers. People with a background in Sociology or Psychology or Education have a different theoretical frame of reference. Although they may be excellent clinicians because of their experience, they will not be admitted to the fold.

There is no point in arguing the merits of this decision. What is important for you to know is that a Master's degree in Sociology or Social Science is not the same as a social work degree. To qualify for certain social work positions, particularly the higher-paying ones, you need the MSW.

How do you find the right program? First of all, your guidance counselor will know which colleges offer the MSW degree. For a complete listing of colleges, you can write to:

Counsel on Social Work Education
1600 Duke Street
Alexandria, VA 22314–3421

Some 400 undergraduate programs in social work and 100 graduate programs are available.

It is an easy matter to narrow down your college choices to a geographical area and then look through the catalogs for colleges that offer the BSW and MSW. If you live in an area where a degree program in social work is not offered, consider an extension program. Many colleges offer extension courses in social work in a locale away from their campus. You can do the first year wherever the courses are given close by, but you will have to commute to the college campus for your second year. The commuting may not be so bad, however; it may amount only to one day a week of classes. The rest of the time, you will probably do a field placement—a job—and that can be right in your hometown as long as you have an MSW supervisor to oversee your work.

How you finance your college degree may be another sticking point. All colleges and universities have financial aid offices, and people there can help you apply for guaranteed loans (that you pay back with minimal interest after graduation) and scholarships.

By the time you are looking toward your MSW you'll be at least twenty-two years old because you will have completed a four-year college course first. For many students those next two years may seem impossible. How can you survive even if you land a scholarship to pay for your schooling? There is still rent to pay and groceries to buy.

Talking to the financial aid office people may give you some ideas. Some students leave school temporarily to work for an agency that agrees to finance their schooling after five years or so of work. They agree to repay the agency with two more years of work, and they receive not only their schooling and books, but a stipend to live on while in school. Other students take advanced placement classes so that they can continue in their present job. The second year of the MSW is required on-campus work, so they have to finish their schooling in the regular program, but many find a *paying* practicum.

Your guidance counselor can be of immeasurable assistance in finding a school that suits you. He or she can also help you figure out how you and your family can pay for your education.

How should you go about choosing a college? First of all, you should be thinking about that when you are a junior in high school, not two weeks before graduation. You need time for you and your parents to visit the campuses, talk to the deans, and get an overall feel for the college. In your junior year start consulting college catalogs. Either borrow them from the guidance office or write to the colleges for them. Consider these variables: how far away the schools are, how much they cost, what courses they offer, and what type of students they attract.

Geography

Consider how close to your family you want to be in the next four years. If you choose a college on the other side of the country, you may be stranded for several months at a stretch. On the other hand, if you choose a school twenty miles up the turnpike, consider whether or not you have really left home.

Consider, too, the environment of the schools. Are they located in the big city, the mountains, or near other schools? If you are a skier it might be fun to go to a college in the mountains where you can spend your weekends skiing. On the other hand, if you select a college for its party atmosphere you may not get much of an education in the long run. If you're shy and don't want to stand out, don't choose a college where your accent will give you away the minute you open your mouth. Geography *is* important; it will help to pare down the number of your possible choices.

Costs

When I selected my undergraduate college I never considered the cost. I simply assumed that my father would pay for it, which he did—for the next ten years. It didn't occur to me until later that he was also paying for my older brother to go to college at the same time. Give your parents a break. When all is said and done and you're working at some agency, it probably won't matter that you went to a preppy New England college at a cost of $20,000 a year. If you choose a college that costs more than you or your parents can easily afford, you won't enjoy the experience because you'll have to worry each semester whether the money is there for you to continue.

Courses Offered

Obviously, it makes no sense to pick a college without checking to see if it offers the degree you want. Courses in social work or elementary education may not be available at a liberal arts college. You may have to go on to graduate school before you can get a good job.

Next consider the size of the classes. Will you be in lecture room–size groups—100-plus kids—or will you have classes of ten to fifteen students? And does that matter? Do you need greater teacher/student interaction or greater anonymity? Catalogs do not specify the size of classes, but they no doubt are related to the size of the college or university. Ask about it in your interview.

Atmosphere

You are going to spend four long years at this school, so be sure to select one where you'll be comfortable. Notice the students when you visit the campuses. Are they relaxed? or decked out in formal attire? Which appeals to you? What is the atmosphere in the library? Is it empty or busy? Where do the students study? Alone in their rooms, in cubicles at the library, or at long tables where there is constant chatter? What about extracurricular events? What kind of games are played? Is there much school spirit, and does that even matter to you?

Consider the academic standards of the school. If you would have a tough time maintaining a good grade point average it may not be the school for you. You need to get into graduate school, and a poor showing during your undergraduate years will not help you do that. Most graduate schools expect you to take a graduate record examination (GRE) to be admitted to a program, but if your grade point average is high enough they will rely on your academic record alone.

Speaking of exams, you will have to take college entrance exams—either the SAT or ACT—to get into college in the first place. If you are not a good test-taker (and not everyone is), consider which schools rely least on the exam scores. Some colleges have a "cut-off point," and anyone presenting scores below that point is not accepted. So, in the end, your test scores may limit your choices.

When you have narrowed down your choices to a few colleges, visit them and arrange for interviews. If the school is not sure about your academic qualifications, a good interview may tip the scales in your favor. When you visit the campus, seek out students in the library or student union and ask them what they like about the school. Most students like to expound on their school—the bad points as well as the good. Listen to them on both counts.

In the end, you will have to set priorities; it's a rare school that will meet all your expectations. Decide what is most important—how close you'll be to home, how much the school costs, or whether you'll get to go skiing on weekends.

Once you have decided on a school and decided on a major—in this case, social work—you still have plenty of leeway about other courses. Aside from a few "fun" courses, you might consider a business course or two and some anthropology courses. The business courses will help if that is the branch of social work you eventually choose, and the anthropology courses will help to give you an overall appreciation of human cultures.

What else can you do in college to give you a head start in social work? Many agencies offer summer intern programs that can give you an idea of the jobs available once you're out in the real world. You will be paid for these internships and can learn at the same time. The contacts you make will be invaluable, too. Sometime soon you'll be looking for work. It's nice to have someone who remembers your work or who will be a reference for you.

But perhaps we have jumped too far ahead. Right now—even in high school—there are things you can do to prepare for social work. Volunteer jobs are a good place to start; you'll get a feel for the work and *you'll be needed*. You can volunteer in nursing homes, in hospitals, or in day-care or senior citizen agencies. Better to find out now if you enjoy working with people in this fashion than to spend a fortune on education first. Furthermore, volunteer work will give you a head start in the job search later on, because you'll be a known quantity with work experience and references.

What if you are not a particularly good student? Can you still get into college? You will have an opportunity to plead your case in the interview or in an essay in the admission application. If your grades were poor in your early years of high school but improved in your later years, you can show that you take your studies more seriously now.

But what can you do right now? You may not have developed good study habits. Organizing your time so that you study more efficiently is the key to better grades. With homework assignments, be sure you know exactly what the teacher wants. Check it out if you're not certain. Tackle your assignments when your energy is up—not at 10 p.m. If you have a lot of homework, break it up into manageable blocks. Do some subjects before dinner and the others after. Reward yourself for completing assignments; take frequent short breaks, but don't get sidetracked watching TV. Make it a habit to do assignments *when they are due.* Some students make the mistake of reading the whole book when only a few chapters are assigned. Then they have no time for their other work. *Do what you can with the time you've got.* Organizing your time simply means establishing priorities. Do the important things first, then those "other" things you enjoy. Always have something fun to do after schoolwork, especially if you consider it boring or hard. Otherwise you'll come to resent your homework and eventually find excuses not to do it.

Since social work is a profession of interaction, it is useful to join groups (Drama Club, sports, 4-H). Groups give you a sense of camaraderie and an outlet for your energy. There are all kinds of ways to "be with people." Just plain having fun is valid, too. You have plenty of time ahead to get serious with your life's work.

Chapter IV

Professional Organizations and Licensure

The most important organization to join if you are a social worker or a social work student is the National Association of Social Workers (NASW). It is expensive (around $130 for professionals, much less for students), but it is of enormous support, and it lends credibility to your name. The NASW publishes a journal every other month and newsletters. You can also purchase liability and life insurance at reduced cost through this group.

Social Work, the NASW journal, can be ordered from NASW, P.O. Box 92180, Washington, DC 20090-2180. The journal costs $51 a year for nonmembers but is free with membership. It publishes scholarly articles on social work policy, theory, and practice. The advertisements alone are instructive; you can find out about workshops and new books. The newsletter carries information on job opportunities around the country, area workshops, and conferences.

Membership in NASW gives you two kinds of support. First, NASW is a nationwide lobbying organization for passage of laws pertinent to social workers. You can express your opinions on such bills and be assured that social workers' best interests will be represented. As a member you also indicate to others that you are a professional, that you belong to a group larger than yourself, and that you adhere to certain standards of professional behavior.

Second, you can attend meetings in your local chapter. Connecting with other social workers for camaraderie and an exchange of ideas is called networking. These people can share job opportunities with you as they crop up.

NASW is an important professional group for social workers. The dues, while hefty to those in lower-paying jobs, are sometimes covered by agencies whose employers require you to join.

Why should social work students want to join NASW? Mostly for the networking opportunities and the information contained in the newsletter and journal. For a nominal fee, student members can participate in their local chapter and get a first-hand look at the social worker experience.

When you move to another state, transferring your membership to another NASW chapter will help you fit into the new social work community.

Another professional organization is the Academy of Certified Social Workers. Members are entitled to use the initials ACSW after their name. As a professional you will have to decide whether membership is worth the expense (approximately $50 a year) and passing the required exam. For many people, it is unnecessary; others want the prestige it carries, indicating that they possess the knowledge and professional experience to have won membership.

In the past five years, board certification has been available for social workers. To apply to be a Board Certified Diplomat of Social Work, you must have five years of postgraduate experience in social work and pass a reportedly rigorous national exam. The benefits of Board Certification, which is nationally recognized and therefore easily transferable to other states— far outweigh the difficulties of taking the exam. There is a fee for taking the exam and for maintaining your certification, as well as a requirement for a number of hours of continuing education credits.

Another aspect of the professional organizations is that they benefit the public as well as the social worker. If an NASW member behaves inappropriately with a client, the group has the power to censure his or her actions. It can do that by canceling membership or openly admonishing the member depending on the seriousness of the misbehavior. By belonging to the NASW or ACSW you agree to abide by a professional code of ethics. If you fail to abide by those standards, you forfeit your right to membership.

Other professional organizations and journals are discussed in the chapters on the various fields of social work in Part 2 of this book.

Other powerful organizations for social workers to join are the hospital unions, which represent the employees' interests in exchange for membership and dues. The dues are relatively small in comparison to the benefits. Don't underestimate the power of a union—even a small one.

Licensure varies from state to state, and you cannot practice social work (and be reimbursed by insurance companies) without it. The reasons for licensure are clear: It certifies that you are qualified for the job, and it gives the licensing board a means of discipline should you betray its standards.

To obtain a license a social worker must have graduated from an accredited school. To receive the title of Social Worker, he or she must possess the MSW degree. Following graduation the person must work for two years as a social worker under supervision of a licensed MSW. During that time the person is considered "license-eligible"; many agencies can hire him or her even though his services are not yet reimbursable by insurance companies. This is mostly an issue for clinical social workers who work in an outpatient facility or in private practice, because agencies lose money if they cannot collect reimbursement on unlicensed personel.

There are at least two national social work exams, and the states specify which one they expect you to pass. If you are a good test-taker and know your field, you should have no difficulty with the exam. It is hard, and the questions are tricky. But after two years of postgraduate work and two years of experience you should be able to answer them. When you apply to take the exam, you indicate an area of specialization in which you will additionally be tested. The choices are clinical social work practice, social work administration, and social work planning and community organization.

The usual license fee is $50. The fee for the licensing exam is an additional $90 to $120. If you fail the exam the first time it costs an additional $90 to $120 to have a second shot.

When you have passed the exam you receive your numbered license and details of all the codes of behavior and rules to which you must subscribe.

Your license is your key to a host of social work positions, so maintain it whether you stay in practice or not. Maintaining your license means renewing it yearly or every other year when it comes up for renewal, and paying the fee.

In addition to the fee for license renewal you have to present credit hours of continuing education in social work—classroom study, workshops, or correspondence courses. Usually the number of hours is 12. The reason for this requirement should be obvious; you need to keep abreast of current theories and research findings to perform an adequate job. Nobody ever stops learning.

Before you wrinkle up your face in disgust, let me assure you that acquiring continuing education credits is not such a bad thing. Workshops, which your agency will probably pay for you to attend, are given in all parts of the country. That means on Cape Cod and in southern California, too.

One of the best workshops I attended was on group therapy, sponsored by the Menninger Foundation. The credentials of the group leaders were impeccable, but the real lure of the workshop was its locale—Aspen, Colorado. My supervisor suspected he was funding a week-long junket for my colleague, myself, and our families, but in all honesty we did learn a lot from our mornings spent in conference.

As I said earlier, licensure varies from state to state. States may not transfer licensure from another state without requiring the applicant to pass their exam. That is what happened to Dwain when we moved back to Oklahoma, where he had originally been licensed six years earlier. Despite his having been licensed in Maine, despite almost fourteen years of clinical experience, the state of Oklahoma still demanded that Dwain pass its test.

I said earlier that you should keep up your social work license even if you are not practicing. It is a small matter to pay the renewal fee, and it's actually fun, or should be, to participate in workshops for continuing education credits. Letting your license lapse, however, and then deciding to get back into social work may mean facing the licensing exam all over again, which is costly and a hassle. If there is any chance that you might return to the profession, you should hang on to your license.

By the way, you can be licensed without an MSW, but a BSW is the very minimum. In that case your license might read: Licensed Social Work Associate instead of Licensed Social Worker, but it is the magic word *licensed* that matters. Go ahead and display your license on the wall of your office; you have earned the right. Being licensed says that you are credible and accountable—and worthy of hiring. If you are Board Certified, too, make sure that information finds its way into every résumé you send out. It says: You're worth it!

Part 2

Overview of Social Work Jobs

Chapter V

Medical Social Worker

Salary range: $23,000 to $40,000 (the higher salaries reflect supervisory responsibilities).

Job Description

A medical social worker works in a hospital and can be assigned to cover any number of wards. If you think of this person as a combination finder-of-resources and crisis worker, you have a good idea of what he or she does. When a patient is admitted, any number of people might decide that he needs to talk with the social worker as well as see the doctor. Let me give you an example. Suppose a thirteen-year-old girl is brought into the emergency room, barely alive from a drug overdose. Of course, the doctors and nurses do their best to resuscitate her and stabilize her condition, but then what? That is where the medical social worker comes in. It is his or her job to assess the girl's drug habit and to arrange to meet with her family so they can decide where she should get help for her underlying problem. A medical hospital can take care of the patient's *physical* needs, but it cannot prolong her stay just because the doctors don't know what else to do with her. It is the social worker's job to locate a drug program (or psychiatric counseling) for the girl and help get her an appointment. If the girl remains suicidal the social worker will consider psychiatric hospitalization and recommend that to the girl, to her family, and to the doctors. As you can see, a medical social worker has to be able to intervene quickly and appropriately in a crisis.

Some patients who are hospitalized because of a stroke or a heart attack need help when they are discharged. Families may not know whom to contact for assistance. The medical social worker knows the resources available in the community and can make the initial call to an in-home nursing service. Not only that, the social worker can meet with the family to discuss the patient's condition and offer emotional support and reassurance.

As you can imagine, the medical social worker's day is never the same, especially if he or she works in the emergency room. In that area one cannot anticipate what services will be needed because the types of patient change from day to day.

If you are good at thinking on your feet, if you are sensitive and caring and not afraid of the pain you will encounter, you would do well here. Naturally, in a hospital you have to face painful situations and on occasion death. Not everyone gets well. As a medical social worker, you cannot afford to become too involved with the patients because then you lose your objectivity. You are with them only a short time before you turn them over to other services. You are a short-term helper, no matter how important.

As a supervisor in the social work department, you do everything just mentioned plus oversee your department (which means making certain that the other social workers are doing their jobs), prepare and manage a budget (because you must decide how much you need for expenses: salaries, workshop and conference money for your staff, and an indigent fund for needy patients), and represent the hospital at community functions. Supervisors are paid a good salary, but they dearly earn every penny.

The medical social worker does not have to see everyone who is admitted to the hospital. Sometimes a doctor suggests seeing one of his patients; sometimes the nurses spot a patient who is depressed or needs "something extra." Social workers themselves routinely go over the list of new patients and those to be discharged, so that they have an idea who might need their services. "So George Henley is being discharged on Thursday. Does his family know the date for the Head Injury Group meeting?" That sort of thing.

Photo 1   A medical social worker checks over her patients' charts.

Even the patient can ask to see a social worker. The medical social worker may need to do some individual counseling before referral to an outpatient therapist. Counseling can include crisis-intervention work (because of child abuse, sexual abuse, or marital problems) and supportive work when someone has just been told he has a life-threatening illness.

The Good Points

If you like working with people and if you have a good idea of community resources (or how to find them), you will like the variety of experiences encountered in this job. A colleague, Sallie Clote, says that she likes her job so much because it's never the same two days in a row.

As in most aspects of social work, it is nice to feel needed, and nowhere is that so readily apparent as in this field. You are able to provide a tangible service, whether that be arranging an appointment for someone to see "somebody else" or finding financial assistance for someone who doesn't realize that any exists for him. In medical social work you see immediate results because you work with the patient only while he is in the hospital. You make the connection for him, and you sit and listen until it is time for him to go. When your service is appreciated, it is hard not to like your job.

As a medical social worker, you work with excellent medical professionals—doctors, nurses, physical therapists. Working around people who are knowledgeable and caring enhances your own experience with the patient.

The Disadvantages

Depending on your point of view, the above list of good points can be turned around and considered disadvantages. You may not *like* having your day unstructured—or structured according to everyone else's needs. You may not *like* running around playing "catch up" with patients who seem to have more needs than you have time for in a day.

Another disadvantage might be not getting to form long-term relationships with patients. Your job is to assist the patient *while he is there* and refer him to someone else upon discharge. Sometimes it is hard to break attachments you have formed, particularly with children.

Working with a variety of personnel means that you will have your share of "difficult" colleagues. They will not all be talented and helpful. Since your job is to interact with the doctors and nurses, it makes for a delicate situation when you have to work with someone you do not like or respect. As a social worker it is not your job to side with a patient against a doctor (unless you do so in the privacy of your supervisor's office). You do not effect change by riling up the patients.

Most people find it hard to work with families whose loved ones are dying, particularly if they are children. It takes a special kind of person to do so on a regular basis, so unless you volunteer for the assignment you probably will not have to deal with it routinely. Nonetheless, you must accept that some of those you try to help will not get better, no matter how hard you will them to live. You cannot take this job home with you, so you learn early to separate their pain from yours. Again, much easier said than done.

And, as a supervisor, my friend warns that the hours are unending.

Degree Requirements

Because this job requires a broad knowledge of social services in the community and the ability to assess and intervene in medical situations, specialization in social work is expected. Most hospitals require the MSW because nowadays more social workers have the degree and therefore the hospital can get them. You may also be asked to be licensed in clinical social work practice or administration (depending on your role.)

Some hospitals have used social workers with only a BSW, but most refuse to accept a person with a nonsocial work degree, even from a related field.

In this position you need the advanced degree and several years of experience for consideration in the larger hospitals.

Opportunities in the Field

States vary in needs and pay scales. Some large city hospitals may be saturated with medical social workers, while rural hospitals may be dying to get even a BSW.

As a rule, however, medical social workers are in high demand. Because of the large number of hospitals, you are practically always sure of a job if you're good. The job tends to have more women than men, although in the supervisory roles you may find a higher percentage of men.

Opportunity for Advancement

Opportunity for advancement means the opportunity to grow into other jobs in the hospital that either require more skills (and hence more pay) or demand more of your time. As a medical social worker your job is on a par with other social workers. The only upward move is likely to be to the head of your department, and that slot is unlikely to open up until the department head leaves. Because hospital social work departments tend to be small (in comparison to the other disciplines), you probably have little chance to advance unless you move into work outside the realm of social work.

Sometimes opportunities for advancement exist in another hospital. When you have established yourself in the field and accumulated some years of experience, you are marketable anywhere.

Opportunities to make more money elsewhere will always present themselves. You then have to decide what compromises you want to make for them. My friend had the opportunity to leave her part-time position in one hospital to take a supervisor's role at another hospital closer to home. She stood to make more money in the new job, and she could walk to work.

However, the supervisor's position was full time so she would have to forfeit some time with her family for the increased benefits and responsibilities.

How to Break into the Job

Medical social workers cannot just walk into a hospital and offer their MSW in exchange for a job. Employers are looking for social workers who have experience in hospital settings or similar agencies. The social workers have to know the resources in the community and possess the skill to work with terminally ill patients, irate families, and suicidal clients. Obviously, the social worker fresh out of college is not a good candidate. In my experience in psychiatric work, the more experienced social worker tends to be the most unflappable. You need to be calm and collected when faced with an emergency or when you run out of resources. Patience and an awareness of the limits to your "giving" seem to come later on in your career. Hospital administrators know that.

If you are interested in medical social work you should begin early to learn as much as you can about hospitals. Volunteer to be a candy striper, or sign on in the summers as a nurse's aide—even in a nursing home. The candidate who already has an understanding of the inner workings of a hospital is that much further ahead in finding future employment.

If possible, select a field placement in a hospital while you are in college. Do an independent study project interviewing a medical social worker to learn firsthand about the job—and for later reference when you are looking for employment.

When you have graduated and received your MSW, apply for a job even if none is currently available. Positions come and go, sometimes rapidly, so it pays to get your name in and check periodically to see where you stand on the list.

In the meantime take a social work job in a community agency—if nothing else to your liking comes along—so that you can familiarize yourself with the resources available in your community. Keep a Rolodex (or file) of names of agencies and their services or of helpful people you come across. You never know when you may need their help again.

Keep your hand in, so to speak, by making yourself known in the community. That does not mean volunteering for every job that comes along in your NASW group, nor does it mean making a nuisance of yourself. It simply means making yourself visible in a professional way. Keep the network open so that you will hear when there is a job opening in your field. And when one comes your way, look back over all your experience (the volunteer work, the community service, the practicums you have held) and put yourself forward in the best possible light.

Helpful Hints on the Job

1. Familiarize yourself with the PDR (*Physicians Desk Reference*) so that you know about medications your patients are using and their side effects.
2. Read health-related journals. A good one to subscribe to is *Health and Social Welfare*, which can be ordered through NASW, 7981 Eastern Avenue, Silver Spring, MD 20910.
3. Keep adding to that Rolodex and periodically check over it. Reestablish contact with people who have previously helped you.
4. Maintain a good relationship with your community sources, including the mental health center. You never know when you might need a favor *fast*.
5. Learn to organize your time right from the start.

Chapter **VI**

School Social Worker

Salary range: $18,000 to $35,000 (depending on locale and size of school system).

Job Description

A school social worker functions much like a clinical social worker except that the clients are usually students. The teacher goes to school to teach her students, and the social worker goes there to help students handle their emotional problems. Naturally, the social worker will not know who will come through the door for help each day unless specific appointments are set up. The crises, of course, cannot be scheduled. The social worker meets with troubled students in a way that guidance counselors are not necessarily trained to do. Often the school social worker has been trained in clinical work (either in a pyschiatric setting or in another counseling agency) so that he or she is prepared to deal with emotionally distraught persons.

What kind of problems does a school social worker encounter? As you can imagine, he or she will probably see students with noticeable behavioral problems. Not necessarily the student who acts up in class once, but the student who repeatedly gets into trouble from smart-mouthing the teacher or hurting other students, including himself. The social worker can explore what is going on in the classroom as well as in the student's home to account for such hostility. What he discovers may lead him to suggest individual counseling with the student, family counseling if the student's parents and siblings seem to be part of his problems, or joint meetings with the student's teachers and the principal. One of my colleagues commented that she felt as if she were constantly "putting out fires."

Working with troubled students is not the whole job, however. Some school social workers routinely work with all the students in special education classes, assessing whether or not their needs are being met. The paperwork to deal with all those students turns into a mountain if you are not careful to write your notes promptly and succinctly.

The social worker also attends meetings regarding the students' academic or emotional needs and even runs workshops with the students to build their self-esteem.

Some social workers handle three or four schools in a city, which does not give them much time to "fit in" anywhere. Running back and forth between schools is no doubt what gave rise to my friend's comment about putting out fires.

School social workers who are assigned to cover an alternative class for the regular school system may find their job better defined. Students in an alternative class are there usually because they did not fit in with the other students or teachers in mainstream classes. They may be seen as troublemakers or underachievers, so the social worker can anticipate some difficulty maintaining the student's interest in school.

Let me tell you a few typical situations I handled as a school counselor in an alternative class. My first crisis was a girl who overdosed on a tranquilizer. She wound up in a hospital after her stomach had been pumped and was later transferred to a psychiatric hospital for treatment of depression. Although she was no longer in my hands, I maintained contact with her to let her know we had not forgotten her.

Another student cut her wrists after a fight with her boyfriend. She received sutures and a night in the hospital, but when she refused psychiatric treatment she was released.

Getting her into the mental health center took most of the next day; I not only had to reassure her family but also convince the girl that therapy was not the end of the world. Perhaps the hardest part was securing an appointment for her at the center when they were booked weeks in advance. In this case I realized my shortcomings as a school counselor: I could not be responsible for a suicidal student; she had to be referred to someone in a psychiatric facility.

Often I had to take a student aside and remind her how important it was to finish school and how close she was to finishing. Sometimes she would be upset over an assignment, sometimes angry over trouble at home. In some cases I had to calm the student down when she was too angry to attend class; in others I had to calm down a parent who was upset with the limitations of our program.

The school social worker does not always handle monumental problems. Sometimes by leaving the door open, he or she encourages students to wander in "just to talk."

Students often came by to see me and started out saying, "I don't have a problem or anything. I just came by to talk."

"Well, have a seat," I'd say, and next thing I knew I was hearing about a boyfriend on drugs, or a mother with a drinking problem, or the student's difficulty finding a summer job.

The school social worker's job, then, much like any social worker's, is defined by the problems of the clientele. In this case: the school system. Sometimes the problems are big and seemingly unmanageable; sometimes finding resources in the community for the student and his family is all that is needed.

The Good Points

If you like an unstructured day and the hustle and bustle of the school setting, you will like this job. Like medical social work, this work never gets boring because *people* never get boring. Your day is your own, which means that you get to decide, more or less, how many students you will see or when you will give your next workshop. If you run out of things to do in a day (rather an unlikely prospect), you can wander into a classroom and feel welcome.

If you enjoy kids in the first place—and that you must do—you will enjoy your work. Helping children sort out their problems (whether you work in elementary school or the higher grade levels) can be gratifying. Kids can be so appreciative.

Photo 2   The school social worker's clients are primarily students—even in elementary schools.

Creating workshops designed to help kids feel good about themselves can be fun too. Most students will respond to your efforts, and that's a nice feeling.

And, of course, you have your summers off. You may receive some of the benefits the teachers get (if you negotiate for them), such as tuition for further education courses and workshops.

The Disadvantages

The bad parts of this job have mostly to do with the extra running around that may be required. You may find yourself without an office, particularly if you cover more than one school. There's little worse than feeling like an official without an official place.

If you have trouble structuring your day you will be at a true disadvantage because you will not have a supervisor standing over you reminding you what you need to. In fact, in most districts you will not have a social work supervisor; you'll be accountable to the school (the principal and superintendent).

Another disadvantage can be feeling that what you have to offer is not appreciated. If you cannot talk freely with the teachers or other staff members, you will feel powerless to effect change for the kids. If you do have that trouble, however, you can usually switch schools for a system in which you are more comfortable.

You will not have the opportunity to socialize with other social workers on the job because very likely you will be the only one. That can be lonely.

The paperwork seems to be a universal complaint, but every profession has mountains of it. You need to make peace with paperwork early in your career, or you'll suffocate under the pileup.

Degree Requirements

Currently the school system itself sets the degree requirements for the job. The larger school districts expect the MSW because they probably can get someone who has it, and because the additional years of experience and study are to their benefit. Other schools employ BSWs or even people with a Master's in a related field as long as they can get state licensure in some capacity. The requirements for licensure are tightening, however, which in essence means that most school systems are moving in the direction of hiring only MSWs.

Opportunities in the Field

There is certainly room for more school social workers, but not all school districts can afford to hire one. This field is increasing in importance, so perhaps in the future the demand will be greater.

Women dominate in this field for two reasons. First, of course, more women hold the MSW degree. Second, it is a great job for a mother with young children. School social workers have the same vacations and school breaks as the teachers, so women like the job because it allows them to be home with their children.

Opportunities for Advancement

The job offers no real upward mobility unless you are assigned to a large school with a social work department. Only then can you aspire to head the department, take increased job responsibilities, and earn substantially more money. Otherwise you may have to look into school districts that pay better salaries, offer more incentives (for example, paying part of your tuition to return to school yourself), or are more conveniently located.

How to Break into the Job

This is another job in which you can increase your worth to potential employers by having a thorough knowledge of your environment. How do you learn about the schools? Volunteer or get hired as a teacher aide or in the Head Start program in your community. In the summer involve yourself in recreational programs, which will bring you into contact with students of all ages.

School districts want people who are supportive of schools in general and have a working knowledge of the classroom. Former teachers thus fit in well. Beyond that, candidates need excellent counseling skills to handle emergencies. A school social worker needs to know when to treat someone and when to back off and refer to someone with more specialized skills. Only the experienced person knows his or her own limitations.

While working on your social work degree, take some education courses, and perhaps spend your field placement or a longer practicum in a school setting.

Get some training in clinical practice (counseling). Familiarize yourself with community resources; you will sometimes need to refer to other agencies and people for assistance beyond what you can provide. Attend school board meetings; these are usually open to the public. The more contacts you make even before you apply for a job, the better. Contacts become resources and potential references; you can never have too many of either. When you think you have sufficient experience and are licensed or license-eligible, apply to as many schools as you can.

You can only find out where the jobs are if you keep your ears and eyes open and let people know you are looking. When I enrolled my oldest child in kindergarten several years ago, I spent some time chatting with one of the guidance counselors there. It happened that the school was looking for a social worker, and she encouraged me to apply for the job—even though I assured her that I was not in the market.

Another way to bring yourself to the attention of the schools is to volunteer to teach a night course or two in the adult education department. You will get minimal pay for teaching these classes (which can include anything from basket-weaving or aerobics to art history), but the point is to get your foot in the door and keep your name circulating in a positive manner.

You want administrators who pick up your job application to say, "Her? Oh, I know who she is."

Helpful Hints on the Job

1. Keep on top of your paperwork.
2. Subscribe to educational journals (or read them in the school library) to keep up with what is going on in the classroom and in educational trends.
3. Maintain your contacts with other agencies and people in the community; you never know when you might need a favor.
4. Stay involved in some physical activity or sport—partly so you'll feel young like those you work with, and partly as a good way to "ventilate."
5. Recognize your place in the system so that you don't find yourself split off from your teaching colleagues.

Chapter VII

Community Organization and Administration

Salary range: As a community organizer, supported by funding grants, you can name your salary (as long as it is in line with similar professionals). In administrative work the salary varies with the size of the agency and whether or not it is privately funded. A reasonable range is $35,000 to $60,000.

Job Description

In this chapter we shall look at the variety of jobs available when you go into community organization or rise in the ranks in administrative work. First let's look at the job of the community organizer.

As the name implies, this social worker goes out into the community and "organizes" things. He or she is not the social reformer who goes around organizing protests. Instead, he or she seeks to define a service that is lacking in the community and demonstrates how to fill that need. Let me give you an example.

When Dwain was in his second year of graduate school he worked out of the Area-Wide Aging Agency. As part of his practicum, he developed a plan to address the needs of the elderly crime victim. First he researched the literature. Then he made his own survey of the types of crime committed and the sites of the crimes. When he had accumulated the data through police reports and crime statistics, he formulated a mission (purpose for his proposal), his goals and objectives, and what it would cost (in funding).

In this case the mission was to find out what types of crime were commited against the elderly and how the police department could better respond. One of the objectives was to educate the police department about the elderly victim's needs. A special police person trained to deal sensitively with victims could be sent to deal with each reported case. At that time there were no policemen who knew how to link the elderly person with community resources in case of burglary, who could counsel the victim or help him reapply for his social security card if it had been stolen.

Another objective was to educate the senior citizens about crimes committed against them and at the same time advise them of the agencies that could respond to their needs. Educating the senior citizen contingent meant speaking to them where they congregated—at senior citizen dinners and recreational centers.

The community organizer, then, must *define a problem* in the community and write a proposal to address that need. The proposal outlines the objectives, how much the mission will cost, and a means of evaluating whether or not the objectives were met.

All kinds of community jobs can be funded through state and federal monies. You need to uncover a need, propose a way to address it, and, of course, know where the dollars are.

Some social workers have tackled community revitalization projects, finding ways to bring a neighborhood back to life and helping the residents do it. You first have to have a plan and the money to see the plan through, and then you have to have the heart to put the words into action. The job calls for diligence and persistence (in digging up facts to support your plans), creativity (in finding resources), and initiative. To remain steadily employed, you either have to keep writing grant proposals or tap into an agency that will continue to fund you because they believe in what you're doing.

One woman I know wondered how libraries funded their expansion. She discovered that library boards of trustees were not particularly adept at organizing expansion. They could not agree on what part of the library to expand or on how to raise funds. Sometimes they had not even assessed the community's needs for library services.

So this woman devised a plan to help library boards learn how to expand their services. She learned all she could on the subject, and through experience helping her own library grow she became a consultant on the subject. People paid to have her show them a way to assess their community's needs for library services and then to fit it into their budget. She had seen a need and met it, following certain established procedures: defining a diagnostic tool (the informal survey) and matching needs with money available for improvements. Thereafter she showed them how to apply for grants and offered fund-raising techniques. As a coordinator for library renewal projects she created her own consulting position.

If you choose to tackle this less easily defined social work position, remember that you must know where the funding money is and be adept at writing grants to get it. You have to be a good salesman, too; excellent persuasive skills are necessary for this job.

What about administrative work connected to community organization? In the recent past it has been discovered that when a group of people get together to do something, the social worker among them usually takes over the leadership role. He or she possesses the skills to organize and supervise. So in community projects social workers are readily made project leaders—and hence, administrators.

Social workers have had much success running programs and even whole agencies. In Norman, Oklahoma, two huge agencies stand side by side. A woman social worker (the first in the agency's 43-year history) is the deputy director of one agency. She is responsible for supervision of the staff, social services, medical records, and the psychology department as

Photo 3   The good administrator is always aware of what goes on in his department.

well as being the school administrator. Next door at the mental health center, another social worker is co-deputy director, responsible for supervising and staffing the whole facility and managing relations between the legislature, the Central Office, and the mental health center. These two social workers head not only their departments but the agencies themselves.

Another colleague does a different kind of administrative job. He works as an auditor for the state, checking the various mental health agencies for compliance with state statutes. His work takes him across the state auditing the agencies' records. The job requires that the social worker have a thorough knowledge of medical records and the diplomatic skills to urge compliance in record-keeping.

Another colleague is the director of outpatient services in a large psychiatric hospital. He has authority over several programs: the outpatient program, transitional living, and partial hospitalization. It is his job to staff and supervise these programs and to coordinate them with the other services of the hospital. It is also his job to promote these programs in the community by attending mental health meetings and conferences throughout the state and the country. An administrator is responsible for everything that goes right (and wrong) in his or her programs, which means being aware of everything that goes on. He or she also has to project a positive image of the organization in the community, so part of the job is "politicking" with important people. An equally important task is educating the general public about the organization's services. The good administrator is not only a good administrator but also a practiced speaker and an engaging personality.

The Good Points

With any one of these jobs you will be attracted to the diversity of tasks. You do not do the same thing every day, even if you have the same responsibilities. *You* decide what needs to be done, and how. You have fewer people to answer to, although, of course, you have to be even more responsive to public opinion.

If you like responsibility, you have plenty. As a community organizer you have the whole responsibility for defining and funding your project. As an administrator you are everyone else's boss and, as such, able to call your own shots. (Of course, there is a down side to increased responsibility.)

You will like also the independence this job offers; you create your own schedule and make your own decisions.

Real incentives to this job are the salary and prestige that come from running an organization. For some people there is satisfaction in running their own show, as the community organizer does. He or she meets interesting people and works with them on a collegial basis to influence change in the community.

There is the satisfaction of having created a program to meet the needs of a segment of the community. When you have done a job well and it is appreciated, you realize why you are in this line of work.

Lastly, you have the opportunity in some of these positions to travel to major cities in the line of duty—which is not to say that you can't make a vacation out of some of the better places. Administration isn't all work.

The Disadvantages

Most of the pluses just mentioned can be disadvantages to some people. Maybe you don't like added responsibility. Maybe you don't like feeling ultimately responsible for anything that goes wrong in the department. With increased responsibilities come increased hours, too. Longer hours, a more serious attitude, and a greater distance to "fall from grace" make this a potentially exhausting job. You need a good deal of energy. One of our friends who is an administrator of a large company walks around work with great strides, his head bent and his shoulders hunched as if he were pushing against a strong headwind.

Then, of course, there is politics to deal with. You not only have to appease the people in your organization but also the important people in the community who support you. You have to be careful not to step on people's toes, not to say the wrong thing. You may be expected to work with legislators on issues that directly affect your agency.

As a community organizer dependent on grants to fund your programs, you always have to worry about the funding sources drying up. If they do, you have to be exceptionally creative and resourceful to compete with a thousand others for that community service dollar.

Degree Requirements

Not only is the MSW necessary for administrative jobs, but you are also expected to have state licensure with specialization in social work administration.

For community organizers it is essential that you have your MSW and broad experience (from your schooling) in social work administration and community organization.

Opportunities in the Field

The field, particularly for community organizer social workers, is dependent on the economic climate. When times are tough and service programs are being cut, it is harder to get funds for projects.

Men and women probably are evenly distributed in these jobs. Men naturally gravitate toward the more financially rewarding positions in the field, and some of those positions are seen as an extension of the corporate world. You need assertiveness, shrewd business sense, and initiative—traits that are traditionally ascribed to men. Women do make good administrators, but as in many professions men seem to rise faster in the ranks.

Opportunities for Advancement

In these positions the sky is the limit for advancement. You can go from supervising your department to running the whole agency or another equally large company.

Community organizers can tackle any size job they put their mind to, and because they write their own budgets and find their own funding sources, they can write their own salaries.

With each project success you establish your credentials so that you can tackle bigger and bigger projects. In the end you may effectively write yourself into a job at a regular agency and then rise to administer that program.

Photo 4 Social workers especially administrators and community organizers—are also good business people.

Opportunities for advancement are limited only by your energy and drive.

How to Break into the Job

You need to specialize in social work administration and planning or community organization when working on your MSW degree. Some people have stepped into administrative jobs directly upon graduation, but that is unusual. Others have created a niche for themselves working on a special community project within an agency and then moved on to administrative work after developing planning skills.

Read everything you can about communities to gain a thorough knowledge of the good ones and the bad—and why. Take some business courses, courses in your department's research methods, and city and regional planning courses. Learn all you can about grant writing and applying for other funding sources. Even as an administrator, you will be expected to bring money into the agency.

If you cannot find a suitable spot right away, take any related position and develop your community proposals in your spare time. Get on the board of some organization in your community. I became a trustee at the library and was suprised how quickly I made vital contacts in the community.

When you have established your name in the community, you can activate your networking. If you don't hear about the perfect job, you may just have to create it.

Helpful Hints on the Job

1. Be professional, because you are highly visible in these roles.
2. Remember your friends and contacts. You got where you are through hard work and other people's support.
3. Learn to manage your time efficiently; otherwise there won't be enough hours in the day.
4. Subscribe to all the pertinent journals.

5. If you "get" from the community, remember to *give something back*.

6. Hold to your principles; they are your most important assets.

Chapter VIII

EAP Social Worker

Salary range: $30,000 up, depending on locale and size of agency. An entry-level position would likely be in the mid-twenties.

Job Description

Employee Assistance Program (EAP) social workers discussed here are the "in-house" social workers who are hired by the organization they serve and are therefore part of the organization. Other social workers provide EAP services that are external to the companies served; they are discussed along with clinical social workers in Chapter 12.

Employee Assistance Programs evolved out of the early substance-abuse field. Managers needed to find some way to help the employee who was no longer doing an effective job because of chronic tardiness, absenteeism, or a poor attitude. Substance-abuse workers (who themselves were usually recovering alcoholics or addicts) demonstrated to employers that the alcoholic employee could be rehabilitated and put back on the job—at a saving to the company, which was losing money because of sick leave costs and the employee's reduced effectiveness on the job. With management behind the programs, the EAPs steadily gained favor; currently some 70 percent of

Fortune 500 companies have EAPs in place. By encouraging the employee to do something constructive about his problem, the companies saved money. If the employee resolved his drinking problem (which was the primary focus in the beginning of EAP work), he returned to his job and presumably became more efficient.

Nowadays the focus of EAPs has broadened to include any personal problems that are causing the employee trouble on the job: finances, the state of a marriage, a family member's drug problems, or legal difficulties. Some in-house Employee Assistance Programs help resolve work-related stress—friction between employer and employee. Many companies believe that if they are going to uncover employee problems on the job (and with mandatory drug-testing more problems are being uncovered), they must have a program to help the employee. Hence the increasing reliance on already-established EAPs.

One part of the EAP social worker's job is to counsel the people he serves. He first does an intake on a person asking for services to decide what type of service is needed. If the EAP social worker cannot provide the service himself—if more in-depth clinical counseling is needed—he or she refers the person to a qualified social worker in the community. Sometimes, however, the EAP social worker continues to provide individual or marital counseling to the employee. Since this service is free to the employee in the work setting, he or she is more apt to take advantage of it.

In addition to counseling, the EAP social worker acts as a consultant to supervisors (or may do so if his job description permits). In this role he offers advice on work-related difficulties with employees and does problem-solving with the supervisors to resolve the crisis with the least disruption. My colleague who is an EAP social worker in a university says that supervisors call him asking for suggestions on how to approach an employee on a work-related issue. My friend recommends addressing the problem *behavior*—not the character of the employee—and then suggests how that behavior can be improved.

A third aspect of EAP work is training other personnel in

better work relations. The social worker does this by preparing and conducting workshops for other in-house staff. (An example might be: How to Manage Difficult People.)

As the EAP social worker becomes recognized in the field, he or she is sought out as a speaker at conferences. Depending on *where* you are asked to deliver your workshop and how you are compensated for the extra job, you may end up with a paid vacation. Dwain was once asked to participate in a workshop conducted in Kennebunkport, Maine. We received free lodging in a topflight hotel overlooking the Atlantic Ocean. I don't remember much about the workshops offered that weekend, but I remember watching the seals frolicking in the harbor at breakfast . . .

EAP social workers also provide job counseling, career counseling, and referral services, even helping an employee to find a good lawyer if that is what is needed most. He or she may be asked to help an employee "fit in better" on the job. Many times a person gets a job without knowing how to conduct himself. He may not know how to dress, how to talk politely to his peers or supervisors, or even how to present himself in public. It is usually assumed that a potential employee knows that stuff. Not knowing it, however, creates stress on the job—for the supervisor, the employee, and all those who work with him. It is then the social worker's job to help, because the supervisor does not have time.

The work of the EAP social worker is usually of a short-term nature unless he has a private practice and can see employees for ongoing clinical counseling. At the workplace, however, the EAP social worker handles a variety of problems, stepping in to smooth things between supervisor and employee so that work can continue.

The Good Points

One of the good points of this job is the diversity of tasks. My friend Shaun Kieran, who works at the University of Southern Maine, told me, "I get to have a lot of fun in this job. I don't

Photo 5   A good social worker is out of his office—working as much as he's in.

just sit in an office doing therapy. That's a small part of what I do."

Your day will not be structured. Although you have to respond to supervisors who contact you about a problem, *how* you respond is up to you.

One of the good things about an in-house setting is that you are observed by everyone in the organization and therefore are more readily accepted than an outsider. If you are good at your job many people will appreciate what you do not only for them, but for the agency as well. You can feel good about the changes you make in the individual and realize that you have helped the organization keep a valued employee.

Seeing constructive changes come about from your efforts is a real plus; being appreciated for them is an added bonus.

You can experience a high degree of success in this job. In part, that is because you deal with high-functioning people. (Someone who has gotten a job is functioning at a higher level than the severely disturbed person who cannot hold a job.) Likewise, you work with people who are more inspired to do something about their problems. Knowing that he risks losing his job if he does not get help, the employee is more seriously motivated than someone who is inclined to quit when the going gets tough.

Another reason you see more success in this job is that some of your successes will be small ones—for example, linking the employee to another service in the community. Nonetheless, every gain made is a success, and you don't feel so drained at the end of the day when you have done something that others appreciate.

Other good points about this job are the salary, which is good, and the opportunities for growth, which are tremendous.

The Disadvantages

If you are not a high-energy person, this is not the job for you. It is not a job where you can sit in your office all day waiting for people and problems to come to *you*. You will have to keep your Rolodex updated with resources in the community. You will have to make yourself visible and get a feel for your organization. People have to know you are *there* before they will come to you for help.

No supervisor will tell you how to do your job. If you cannot structure your own day you will not enjoy this job—nor will you be good at it.

Problem-solving (which is an art) can be tiring, especially when you are working with people (supervisors or employees) who see no need to change. You *will* have failures in this work, as in other clinical work, and part of handling the job is learning to accept that you cannot help everyone.

Some people worry that office politics will make EAP work unpleasant—that management will not appreciate your efforts if they think you always consider *them* the problem. According to my friend in this field, politics rarely is as troublesome as social workers fear it will be. Most organizations realize that the EAP worker is performing a needed service that is cost-effective in the long run.

The paperwork and the hours may seem onerous, but there is plenty of paperwork in all social work positions, and the hours are what you choose to spend. If you spend more than is stipulated in your contract, either you are not working efficiently or there is more work than one person can handle. If you start accommodating a company that wants 50 hours of work for 40 hours' pay, you are setting a dangerous precedent.

Degree Requirements

Believe it or not, there are no special educational require-ments *at this time*. That is likely to change before you get out of college, however, because all professional jobs are requiring greater specialization these days.

Because the original EAP workers were substance-abuse counselors who were recovering from their own addiction, they seldom had specialized degrees in counseling. As the program broadens to include tasks outside the realm of drug and alcohol abuse, candidates with experience in clinical counseling are needed. Increasingly, MSWs are filling the void because of their systems approach and greater knowledge of community resources.

The Employee Assistance Professionals Association has its

own credentials. It offers licensing as a Certified Employee Assistance Professional by spending so many thousands of hours of certified supervision (which means working in apprenticeship with a Certified EAP), and passing a national exam. Common sense suggests that you need clinical experience, and that comes through working in a psychiatric setting (a hospital or an agency) where you need an MSW. Save yourself time and regrets by getting the Master's degree at the outset.

Opportunities in the Field

In-house EAP jobs are on the rise as companies discover how economical they are. Therefore, the field is not saturated, even though the mental health agencies and private clinicians may have a hold on the external EAP programs. However, the jobs are not always advertised.

Women dominate in this area only because more women have MSWs. It is likely, however, that men will gravitate to the field when they realize the challenges it offers as well as the lucrative salaries.

Opportunities for Advancement

Depending on the size of the company or organization, this job offers some potential for advancement. If you are part of a large Human Resources Department you can move up the ladder to take over the department.

Otherwise the opportunities for advancement are lateral. You can move to another company for more money or prestige, but within the corporation there is no way up unless you move into another line of work.

How to Break into the Job

Most EAP jobs are not listed in the newspapers because companies like to have a candidate in mind even before they establish their in-house program. That is where networking is important. If you have gotten your name around in the community and are well thought of, you may be consulted about a job before you know a job is being offered.

However, this is *not* an entry-level job in which candidates fresh out of college can be effective. You need to "pay your dues," so to speak, by gaining clinical experience, and one of the best places to do that is in a psychiatric setting. Working in a counseling agency is instructive, but the fastest way to pick up clinical skills is in a psychiatric hospital. Working in an admissions area, assessing the problems that come through, and dealing with the more severe forms of mental illness will help you hone your skills. In hospital work you also learn how to behave professionally. When you have acquired some experience (and that includes diplomatic skills), you can activate your networking leads to discover the right EAP job.

Work in a personnel agency while in school, or in addition to any social work job you may have. In that way you can start out with a knowledge of how organizations work and the Human Resources Department in particular.

Even if you have your MSW degree, you might consider an apprenticeship program with a Certified Employee Assistance Professional. You will end up with your CEAP certificate and many job leads.

Know your material. Read not only about EAPs but organizational structure. Take some business courses. Find out why Lee Iacocca turned his organization around, and why Trump fell out of favor.

Helpful Hints on the Job

1. Read all the EAP journals you can get your hands on. Some are expensive, so see if your company will order them for your department. Here are some choices:

   EAP Association Exchange (monthly)
   EAP Association, Inc.
   4601 North Fairfax Drive

Arlington, VA 22203
Employee Assistance (monthly)
225 North New Road
Waco, Texas 76710

EAP Digest (bimonthly)
Performance Resource Press
2145 Crooks Road
Troy, MI 48084

2. Get to know the company's supervisors, and don't assume you are there only to address the "little man's" needs. Be careful not to prejudge *any* situation.
3. Practice professionalism; respect confidentiality.
4. Keep your Rolodex of community resources active. Maintain your old contacts and consistently make new ones.
5. Enjoy your work; if you don't, what's the point?

Chapter **IX**

Family Planning Clinic Social Worker

Salary range: $15,000 to $28,000, depending on the agency's funding sources and your credentials and experience. Private agencies, as a rule, pay more.

Job Description

The social worker can perform numerous tasks in a family planning clinic. Obviously, a great part of her day is spent providing reproductive information to families and counseling people for whom pregnancy is an unwanted or (at the very least) unexpected event.

Entry-level social workers (or students fulfilling their practicums) administer the pregnancy tests and provide information about pregnancy and health care should the tests be positive. More experienced social workers with clinical skills provide the follow-up counseling if the pregnancy is not a welcomed event.

Family planning agencies vary in their stance on abortion. In some agencies (especially those with a religious affiliation) the social workers do not consider abortion for clients; if a client seeks that specific information they urge her to reconsider such a drastic move. In other agencies social workers present all alternatives to pregnancy, leaving the decision to the client.

Dealing with teenage clients in a highly charged emotional situation has to be carefully done. Because many clients are under eighteen, and because some communities object to having abortion information given to anyone, the family planning social worker needs to be sensitive to opinions in the community. You should know your own values first and foremost. The social worker cannot direct people to do things she considers unethical.

Before researching this chapter I thought the "good" social worker presented all the alternatives equally. I thought the good social worker was nonjudgmental and adhered to the philosophy put forth in the NASW Code of Ethics. A colleague, however, had a different approach to the issue. Because she values the life of the fetus as well as the pregnant woman, she believes she must state her position to the client upfront. Not to advise against abortion is against her philosophy.

Whatever your position, you must believe in what you are doing. Whether you are pro-choice or anti-abortion, you must maintain your compassion for the client who has to make the decision. What impressed me most about my colleague who advised against abortion at her clinic was that she continued to work with those clients who nonetheless went elsewhere for the abortion. She found that no matter how prepared the woman was for ending the pregnancy, she still felt pain at the loss. The pain may not flare up immediately, but years later, when something happens to remind the woman of her previous loss (perhaps another pregnancy or an anniversary date), she is surprised at the hurt from the original loss. In response to that need, this family planning social worker offers a post-abortion recovery group, a twelve-week program that allows the woman to get in touch with her loss and make peace with herself for having precipitated it. This support group seeks to heal the woman, not blame her.

The family planning social worker, then, counsels all clients and refers some to other parts of the health community if necessary. Sometimes she recommends doctors; sometimes she helps a young girl tell her parents that she is pregnant. If an unwed young mother-to-be needs shelter or financial help, the social worker assists her in connecting with those resources. If the client wants to give her child up for adoption, the social worker provides ongoing counseling to be sure that the woman is emotionally prepared for that experience. Some agencies offer an Adoption Support Group for women in all stages of the adoption process.

Photo 6   Part of the Family Planning social worker's job is counseling and referral.

Sometimes this social worker provides longer-term counseling for a client who seems particularly at a loss how to deal with her pregnancy. Clients exhibiting severe signs of mental disorder are referred to the appropriate mental health facilities, but the family planning social worker provides ongoing counseling to many clients because her services are usually free.

Apart from counseling, the social worker sometimes instructs her clients about their pregnancy (how to care for themselves, how to care for their newborn baby, how to handle the surprises of labor and delivery) and oversees foster home families who support the agency.

At one agency the head of the department created and managed an outreach program for rural clients who could not come in for family planning services. She arranged to have a social worker visit these young women, making sure they knew that they could finish their education in an alternative program if not at their regular high school. She referred some to Human Services and provided guidance for others regarding care of the newborn.

Some social workers run homes for unwed mothers and programs to link foster families with either pregnant teenagers or temporarily with their babies. The social worker is responsible for matching the families and monitoring their care.

Some social workers who start out in these clinics eventually create their own program, funded by the parent agency or through special community grants. One woman set up her own alternative high school for teenage mothers, staffing it with licensed teachers, school nurses, and day-care providers.

The Good Points

This job is never boring either, because people come in all shapes and sizes and with all kinds of problems. You have so many tasks to accomplish at any given time that you should have no opportunity to get bored.

Working closely with families struggling with major decisions can be gratifying when you succeed in helping them. Successes can be small, but nevertheless satisfying. All some people need is information. Some need advice; some need referrals. These services should be easy to supply, and your efforts will be appreciated.

Helping to develop a more responsible person and a more caring parent is gratifying too. If through your efforts a person learns to cope with her predicament you will feel good about your contribution.

The Disadvantages

Because you work in stressful situations, this work can be tiring. The small successes make this giving "tolerable," but it is the distress and failures that may shorten your time spent in this kind of work. Being around so much pain is energy draining.

Dealing with the political repercussions of some of your informational services (particularly abortion referrals) is also draining. I don't think people who go into this line of work do so with the intent to take a forceful stand on any one issue, but sometimes that is what happens.

The pay is low, relatively speaking, unless you manage the agency and assume additional roles. If you do not provide direct services, it means overseeing the volunteers or other social workers who do and being ultimately accountable for their actions.

Degree Requirements

For some of these jobs you can be a volunteer (while working on your MSW or BSW degree), but because of the nature of the work you are well advised to obtain your MSW. Many students opt to spend their practicums here, gaining experience and consultation, learning how to integrate what they hear in the classroom with what goes on in the real world.

For those in counseling positions (where good clinical skills are needed), the MSW is required. Those with BSWs can run some of the support groups. Some agencies require the MSW and state licensure anyway. Since all social work positions are moving toward specialization, the candidate for family planning social worker would be wise to get as much education as possible. If she decides to add other aspects of social work (for example, teaching courses in social work and supervising practicum students), she will definitely need the MSW degree and licensure.

Opportunities in the Field

These jobs are often filled by new social workers or volunteers (still in school), so there may be more social workers who can do the work than there are funds or positions.

As you can probably guess, disproportionately more women fill these roles than men.

Because the pay is relatively low, there is considerable turnover as entry-level social workers gain experience and move on to jobs with more challenge and financial compensation.

Opportunities for Advancement

Since social workers can start in entry-level positions and sometimes as volunteers, there is plenty of room to advance. As you gain experience and the necessary credentials, you can move into counseling roles and advance eventually to an administrative role if your agency is of sufficient size.

Some social workers combine other aspects of social work and write grant proposals to fund their own projects. Branching out in this capacity—being a consultant as well as an organizer—can be rewarding both financially and personally.

How to Break into this Job

This job is easier to access than some other social work positions because agencies offer entry-level jobs. You can probably walk into a job right out of college if you have the right credentials and some experience in family planning work.

You can gain the experience either by doing your practicum and placements at these agencies or by volunteering during vacations and school breaks. Some tasks, such as administering pregnancy tests and making referrals to other agencies for services, you can do right from the start.

If you want to spend more time in counseling, brush up on your clinical skills first. Work in close supervision with another MSW, or work at a hospital, honing your clinical and assessment skills.

Keep your network channels open. Sometimes these jobs are filled by word of mouth.

If you cannot find a job to your liking right away, take another satisfactory position (even if it is unrelated), but volunteer at one of these agencies in the meantime. Perhaps when an opening occurs the staff will offer it to you because they are familiar with your work.

Helpful Hints on the Job

1. Respect the client's confidentiality at all times.
2. Respect the values of your agency. If you cannot condone some of their practices, it is best not to work there; compromising your values to make a living will eat away at your self-esteem.
3. Read everything in the field. Ask your agency to subscribe to the major journals, or order them yourself.
4. Stay on top of community resources; like information, resources are always changing.

Chapter **X**

Instructors in Social Work

Salary range: $28,000 to $70,000, depending on the college or university and on your experience and credentials.

Job Description

Since social work is not a subject taught in high school, this chapter addresses college level instructors.

Depending on the size of the college and its social work department, an instructor is responsible for any number of tasks. First and foremost, the instructor has to prepare the course, deliver the lectures or lead the discussions, devise a way (usually a test or essay) to assess what the student has learned, and then grade the work. Readying yourself to teach a course in social work is no easy matter. You have to know your subject, and that means immersing yourself in it so that you have more information than what is in the textbooks. Sometimes you may be able to choose the textbooks for the course. But teaching goes beyond knowing the material. It requires the ability to make the subject understandable to others. Thus you need to be part entertainer and part disciplinarian.

To be a good instructor, you must be open to even more learning. You spend a great deal of time at first getting to know your students, because the better rapport you have with them, the easier it is to engage them in class. Administering tests and grading papers takes a lot of time.

Part of social work instruction is monitoring work practicums, coordinating placements in the community, and getting input from the supervisors under whom the students work. (Not all instructors fill this role, however.) As a field instructor, you continually have to drum up "good" placements; you spend a lot of time checking in with the supervisors and monitoring the student's work. If problems crop up it is your job to smooth them out. Whether that means taking the student in hand or helping the supervisor to get along better with the student, it calls for diplomacy.

Part of an instructor's job is to promote the image of his college or university, and that means committee work, "hobnobbing" with the public (to generate community support), and attending university functions (which can be things like sports events and the arts.)

Many instructors act as counselors, although that is not their designated role. Good teachers always do more than teach; they sometimes sit down with students and help them sort out their troubles so they can get on with their studies. Instructors have occasion to refer students to the school's counseling center and to advise them on many subjects outside their realm. Dwain had a college instructor who invited his whole class home for dinner and "discussions" afterward in political science.

Some instructors help a student decide what he wants to do with his life. It may be easier for the student to talk to a teacher he trusts than to a guidance counselor he considers a stranger.

When instructors are noted in their field they may be asked to speak at organizations or to conduct workshops in their field of expertise. You need to perfect your speaking ability because you cannot rely on your authority as a teacher to carry you through these large gatherings. Nowhere is a sense of humor more appreciated. People who attend workshops want to learn something, of course, but they also want to be entertained. A good instructor can do both.

The Good Points

Being an instructor offers you independence (although you still have to conform to your school's policies) and challenge. You work with idealistic young students who typically want to change the world, and their enthusiasm is catching at times.

You get to talk as much as you like and have the satisfaction of seeing people take notes on what you say. You are an authority figure, and others look up to you (assuming you have earned their respect.) You direct the flow of the classroom and create your own evaluation tools. Being appreciated and remembered fondly—what greater pleasure than that?

You are well paid as a rule, and you have the opportunity to travel, attending workshops. You have ample breaks in your schedule and a lengthy summer vacation. If you are a tenured professor you have periodic sabbaticals when you can use a whole semester (with pay) to go somewhere else and research your next book—or teach in another university.

Being an instructor has numerous "perks." Your children can attend your college either at a reduced fee or free. Other colleges may offer reduced fees to your children as a professional courtesy. You have the opportunity to influence the direction of your department and to make a lasting contribution in your field of specialization.

The Disadvantages

Now the bad stuff: You have to be prepared to *teach* each class, even when you don't feel like preparing a lecture the night before. It takes a lot of time to prepare a lecture and to study enough other material to remain an authority on the subject. Not only that, you have to devise tests and course assignments and read papers when they are handed in. That takes a substantial amount of time. Fairly assessing someone's work—making relevant notes in the margins—takes time, and the only time you have is after hours, when the students have gone home and you're thinking about a relaxing evening.

Students will expect you not only to make the course understandable, but also *entertaining*. They expect you to be knowledgeable, funny, and as idealistic as they are. Because you are an authority figure, they will reject some of what you say, and they will tire of hearing what the real world is like.

Your hours extend far beyond the classroom. You have to explain the systems theory to a student for the umpteenth time because he just hasn't "gotten" it. You have to calm another student who thinks she's going to flunk your research and methods course. And you have to stand firm when still another student suggests that you gave him a C- on his exam because he is foreign and you are prejudiced.

If the students don't wear you down, the politics of the department just might. Trying to teach a subject while being sensitive to the public image of the college can be tiresome. Some instructors say that committee work is the most boring aspect of their job.

Degree Requirements

In this profession you need two types of degrees. At the minimum, of course, you need the MSW degree. With that you are eligible to teach in some junior colleges (two-year programs of study) and some of the smaller colleges. In a major university, however, you need both the MSW and the PhD (or DSW). Instructors in the larger universities usually hold PhDs, because teaching requires greater and greater specialization.

Opportunities in the Field

My sources tell me that the need for instructors in social work is great. As usual, more women are visible in the field. However, as many males as females earn PhDs, so the profession of teaching in the larger universities is probably evenly divided between the sexes.

No matter what people say, men still rise faster within the

ranks, perhaps because they do not have the interferences that women face during the childbearing years.

In teaching, as long as you have the right credentials you can usually find a job, although you may have to relocate for it. Then, as you demonstrate your capabilities, you can either find a more secure position in another college or be accepted as an assistant professor and then professor in your current school.

Opportunities for Advancement

As long as you are willing to go as far in your education as you can—obtaining your PhD (which means an additional two to three years beyond your MSW)—you have plenty of opportunity for advancement. One starts out as an instructor at a college or university, then rises to assistant professor, full professor, and tenured professor (which means not having to negotiate a contract each year). If you cannot rise any higher at your current university you can look elsewhere; as long as you are willing to relocate you have plenty of choices available.

As long as you are an effective teacher, publish something of professional interest every few years, and maintain an untarnished public image, you can stay in the field for as long as you choose, perhaps even heading the department if the chance presents itself.

How to Break into this Job

You can break into this field in one of three ways. First, you can make a name for yourself even while you're in school, working on your Master's degree and teaching courses in the undergraduate program. As you work on your PhD (at the same university) you can teach Master's-level courses so that when you graduate and are ready to start teaching full time the school is familiar with your work and may have an opening for you right then and there.

A second way is to take a regular social work job once you

have your MSW and learn all you can about a certain position (for example, clinical social work). After a period of time you return to school for an additional degree (the PhD or DSW) to enable you to parlay your practical experience and your degrees into a teaching position. Someone who has actually worked in the "real" world has more to offer than someone with only book knowledge, how ever grand that might be.

A third way is to get all your education upfront but then go directly into a profession. While you're working as a social worker—no matter what kind—you can sign on to teach "supplemental" courses in social work at night, for example. That may mean teaching introductory-level courses, but as you gradually make a name for yourself and free up more of your time, you can make the transition to full-time teaching if the opening arises.

If your goal is to teach (and believe me, most people *choose* to go into this profession; they don't end up teaching because they couldn't do anything else), you should take as many educational courses as you can fit into your schedule. Take a Dale Carnegie course to improve your speaking ability (and your assertiveness). You have to be able to sell yourself to get the job in the first place and to keep classroom attention.

Volunteer to teach a Sunday School class while you're a student; you'll get a feel for holding kids' attention and some sense of how to plan lessons (even those you don't have to grade.)

Talk to your college instructors; make friends with them because they can give you valuable ideas on how to pursue your goals, as well as act as references later.

Having myself taught classes in Sociology (a related field) and been a clinical social worker, I think you have far more to offer the student if you have been out in the real world, seeing how the social worker lives and works, before you attempt to teach others what it's like.

Applying for a position, putting yourself (your credentials and experience) in a positive light, and calling in those references will eventually land you a good job.

Helpful Hints on the Job

1. Never allow yourself to grow stale teaching; always keep learning yourself.
2. Make yourself available to the students; that's what you're there for.
3. Realize the limits of your job; you don't have to be a counselor if you don't have the skills.
4. Stay in touch with the fields you teach; nothing is worse than presenting yourself as an authority if you really aren't one.
5. Support your college and your colleagues by attending school functions. And enjoy yourself; if you don't (as I've said before), *what's the point?*

Chapter XI

Human Services and Corrections Department Social Worker

Salary range: $15,000 to $28,000. The higher figure re-presents salaries for administrators or department heads.

Job Description

I could devote a whole book to this aspect of social work alone, so broad and varied are the jobs in the Human Services Department. Years ago the traditional social worker in this department did *all* the jobs in his designated locale. When I worked as an intern for the Department of Health and Welfare, I handled clients who were awaiting their monthly AFDC checks; I assisted other social workers in removing children from homes considered temporarily unfit; I sat in on court sessions where a child's custody was being disputed; and I reviewed families who were applying to be foster parents. Any welfare business that occurred in the area fell into my domain. I was the trusty welfare social worker who trekked around meeting my people in their homes.

That has mostly changed. Even as I was returning to school after my internship, the rules were changing. Now social workers specialize in certain *tasks*, which means that some people handle adoption procedures, some handle foster families, and some handle juvenile services. In almost all agencies (with the possible exception of small rural agencies that have retained the traditional social worker's tasks), you have a specific job to perform in the Human Services Department. Human Services is the largest social service agency in each state, and the social workers there are responsible for coordinating all state family services and the lives of thousands of welfare recipients.

If you work in adoption services you are responsible for coordinating the paperwork that goes along with giving a child up for adoption as well as offering short-term counseling to the mother who is relinquishing her parental rights. It means overseeing the adoption court procedures, assessing the emotional and physical health of the prospective parents (as well as their resources), and following up on both families once everything has been signed and agreed upon.

In this agency, you do not handle one case at a time; the Department of Human Services is always swamped with families needing services. You handle scores of cases, all in various stages of development.

The same thing is true if you work in foster care placement. You typically have an unwieldy caseload. You have the unpleasant task of separating families, even those who can't stand to be around each other. For most kids, even the worst parents are better than brand-new strangers. Most children resist being taken (even temporarily) from their home and placed in foster care. I remember helping another social worker who had to transport three children under the age of twelve to a foster home while their mother was hospitalized for surgery. Since the new home would be calmer and had loving parents, I wasn't prepared for the protests that filled the back seat of our car. The kids didn't care that they'd be getting their own rooms and a pile of toys. All they knew was that they were being taken from their home—even though their mother was not necessarily considerate or loving.

In foster care work you also have to follow up on your support families, those people who agree to take in foster kids. It is your responsibility to be sure they are adequate substitute parents themselves and that they are using the state's money to support the foster children, not themselves. You spend time assessing families, matching needy children with potential parents, and attempting to keep the paperwork pileup to a minimum. You may get to do some individual counseling with foster children, but you should not consider yourself a clinical

Photo 7   The   Human   Services   social   worker   is   part   of   a   huge organization—a network of services.

social worker. You may be expected to refer a person to a mental health center for counseling—and then provide transportation to appointments.

Some social workers specialize in court-related community services, acting as probation and parole counselors with juveniles. In this job the social worker (or caseworker, as he or she is sometimes called) offers in-home counseling to the adolescent and his family, accompanies the offender to court, makes reports to the judge, and helps to place some adolescents in private or state facilities as needed.

Some social workers focus on helping recipients of welfare assistance to develop job skills and eventually become employable. Although social workers do not make the routine "home visits" they formerly made, they still make periodic visits to the clients' home to make sure they are "playing by the rules" and are at least adequate parents.

Some social workers have the difficult job of investigating child abuse—verifying that abuse has occurred (which means following up on all reports of abuse), rescuing the child from the home, and then representing the child's interest in court.

Other social workers perform similar functions as case managers in the Department of Corrections. Their duties include providing individual counseling, group therapy, and family therapy to inmates in prison; directing the inmates in their daily activities; approving passes into the community if the inmate is at the appropriate level; monitoring doctor's appointments; and arranging transportation for shopping trips and other appointments.

The caseworker makes pardon and parole appearances, acts as disciplinarian when a major rule violation occurs, and makes sure documentation is current and accurate. A colleague who has held this position says, "The inmates have a level system, and they know exactly what is expected of them, but one of the reasons people come to prison is that they break society's rules. Most of the individual counseling is spent confronting the behaviors that brought them to prison or confronting the behaviors that have prevented them from moving up a level or resulted in their getting dropped a level. Group therapy focuses on value clarification and positive reinforcement; family therapy focuses on establishing a support system for the inmate and setting goals for release. If the family refuses to be involved, or if they are unable to be involved because of distance, the inmate is linked up with community resources for additional support.''

In all these jobs you develop your assessment and referral skills. You do not do in-depth clinical counseling, however; that job is better reserved for the clinical social worker (who is discussed in the next chapter).

The Good Points

These jobs are offered to the entry-level social worker, so while you are not necessarily paid a lot, you at least have a job. Another plus: These jobs are relatively easy to transfer into if you move to another state.

Many of the jobs are gratifying. Not only are you doing work that is needed in the community, but many people are actually appreciative of your efforts. You have the opportunity to make a difference in people's lives and sometimes to intervene in life-threatening situations. The successes justify the headaches.

You get to hone your assessment skills, because you are expected to perform a variety of tasks in addition to the referrals you make. The knowledge you acquire from this job will help you in all your other social work positions if you choose to move on into another area.

Like so many other social work jobs, this one won't get boring (although part of the excitement might come from the danger in some assignments).

The Disadvantages

Many of these jobs offer some degree of danger. People do not always appreciate your services, particularly when you intervene in their lives, telling them what they can and cannot do. Of course, the law is on your side, but some people still won't care. In some areas you will be considered brazen for sticking your nose into private affairs. There are still people who believe that whatever they do in their own family (including beating the kids) is none of your business. When you work with criminals and abusive personalities, you run the risk of being hurt yourself.

Except for administrative positions, these jobs are low-paying, and the only "perks" (if they can be so considered) are travel expenses, paid at so many cents per mile. Those miles really have to add up before an expense check becomes profitable.

Then, too, you will have more people seemingly "against" you than "for" you. Your supervisors will be on your back, so to speak, to hand in your paperwork and document your transactions. At the same time, the public tends to blame the Department of Corrections or Human Services for whatever goes wrong in the handling of clients.

And, as always, the hours can be long, the bonuses non-existent, and the paperwork mountainous.

Degree Requirements

Because many of these jobs are entry level, you can probably start out with only a BSW or a BA (or MA) in a related field. (A related field means any of the social sciences or people-oriented professions.)

The middle-level jobs and, of course, administrative positions require greater specialization, which means an MSW. My sources tell me that to do an official home study in the Human Services Department, you have to have your MSW degree.

Although these jobs currently do not all require the advanced degree, it is worth pursuing anyway. You might take an entry-level job and then arrange for the department to send you back to school for the MSW. Human Services in particular spends a great deal of money sending its people for advanced training, which—come to think of it—is one of their good points. You don't have to repay the money spent on your education; you merely have to put in two more years of service (for which you'll be paid, of course.)

Opportunities in the Field

Turnover is high in these positions, which are often used as springboards to other jobs. There may be a good number of caseworkers for every job, but the chance of being hired eventually is good if you are persistent and patient.

Again (and you're probably tired of hearing this), the field is saturated with women because they make up the bulk of those with the MSW degree. Unfortunately, women tend to take the lower-paying jobs, perhaps because they are easier to come by or because they are more tolerant of the single mother's "handicaps." Women have traditionally been the "social workers" (the helpers), so it is not surprising to find so many still performing that function. Men, however, are a welcome addition to the force.

Opportunities for Advancement

Opportunities for advancement are plentiful (mostly because you are starting at the bottom). Also there is an enormous range of jobs in both departments. If you rise to head any department, you then have the opportunity to branch out into administrative work in other agencies and organizations.

How to Break into this Job

For all of these state jobs you have to pass a state merit exam in addition to meeting the degree requirements. When you have your educational experience, you sign up for a variety of social worker I or II positions (whatever level you qualify for) at the state employment (or personnel) office and then take the scheduled exam.

At the state personnel office you'll find a huge book detailing all the state positions and the degree requirements for each. All you have to do is pick out the job that interests you. When you have passed the exam, your name goes onto a register in order of grade. When you're high enough on the list your name is offered to various supervisors to interview for an opening. You can increases your chances for an interview by getting in touch with various employers yourself, but don't make a nuisance of yourself in this respect.

It helps to do your practicum here, or to work during the summers even in a clerical capacity. The idea is to make yourself known—and indispensable—to the agency so that you will be considered for any appropriate job opening.

Helpful Hints on the Job

1. Respect your clients' dignity. Being needy and desperate makes us all behave badly at times.
2. Keep checking on the state jobs available. Openings come up frequently, and sometimes the person who gets to the supervisor first gets the job.
3. Be sensitive to the politics in your department, and keep documentation of cases current and accurate.
4. Stay on top of your paperwork right from the start.
5. Do your best no matter what your job is. No one will be interested in hiring you for a "better" position if you have not demonstrated that you can handle this one.
6. Remember that you are performing a vital service, even if it does not seem to be appreciated. You *are* needed, and you should be proud of your contributions.

Chapter XII

Clinical Social Worker/
The Therapist

Salary range: $18,000 to $45,000 (depending on whether your agency is privately funded). Social workers in private practice charge $75 an hour for individual counseling in many areas.

Job Description

There are innumerable components of clinical social work. Nonetheless, let us take a quick look at some of the tasks and responsibilites of the inpatient social worker (who works in a psychiatric hospital), the outpatient social worker (who works in a mental health center or private clinic), and the social worker in private practice.

The inpatient social worker in a psychiatric hospital has responsibility for coordinating most aspects of patient care. He or she provides the individual counseling (the initial assessment of whether or not hospital admission is needed) to patients, group therapy to all patients on the ward, family therapy or marital therapy to patients' support systems, and eventual referral to outside agencies for follow-up when patients are released from the hospital.

When I worked at Jackson Brook Institute (a private psychiatric hospital in Maine), I worked with only five patients at any given time. Perhaps you think that does not sound like much work, but responsibility for those patients meant attending daily doctor rounds and weekly treatment plan meetings (where the staff gets together to put on paper how to treat a case); filling out reports; monitoring the medicine regimes of the patients (noting whether and how symptoms were subsiding); contacting family members (and in some cases encouraging them to come in); and either talking to outpatient therapists who had worked with my patients or finding someone new who would work with them upon discharge. All said and done, I spent 40 to 45 hours a week doing my job, between the direct service to the patients and the paperwork.

Speaking of paperwork, you have to write initial evaluations and a treatment plan (detailing the specific condition you are treating, how you are going to treat it, and how long it should take). Along with these reports, you have to compile an individual and a family history. When the patient stays beyond ten days you have to write another treatment plan indicating why the patient still needs to be hospitalized and offering another discharge date. When the patient is released you have to write a discharge summary of what transpired in the hospital and where the patient is being referred for outpatient care.

Although the nursing staff takes care of the patient's day-to-day medical needs, as the clinical social worker you are primarily responsible to oversee his care. Granted, the doctor is ultimately responsible, but he or she delegates this supervision to you, the clinician. The doctor relies on you to report any crisis in the making.

The outpatient social worker has similar responsibilities in that he or she has to fill out the same forms: initial evaluations, treatment plans, and discharge summaries. However, you do not work with the most severely disturbed patients unless it is to refer them to a psychiatric hospital. If you are employed as a case manager, you probably do a lot of work in the community itself, checking up on chronically ill mental patients who are no longer in the hospital. You actually "manage" these clients, because they do not necessarily know how to take care of themselves. That means you have to make sure they are taking their medicine, keeping their other appointments, eating well, and receiving their social security disability checks. If they live in a boardinghouse, you need to check with the operator to make sure she is taking proper care of your clients or to hear

Photo 8   The social worker in private practice is a good listener, *among other things.*

her complaints if any. As a case manager, your job is to help keep the former patient in the community, and to do that you have to monitor all aspects of his or her life and beef up any support systems that may exist for him. (The more supports that are in place for the client, the less direct services you have to perform.)

Otherwise outpatient social workers act much like the social worker in private practice. You job is to see clients (with a variety of problems) in fifty-minute sessions, providing individual, marital, or family therapy. Counseling is not simply "giving advice." It means listening to the client and helping him or her sort through emotions to find a solution to his problems or to find "peace of mind." It does not always happen quickly. People may come to you so depressed that they want to commit suicide but don't have the energy. People may come to you because they have just lost their job, their spouse, or their boyfriend or girlfriend. They come because they cannot sleep (or they sleep too much); they get stuck thinking the same old thought day after day and can't get anything done; or they come despite being terrified to step outside their door. (Those are only a few of the reasons pushing people into therapy, but you get the idea.) Sometimes you will need to refer your client to a psychiatrist because you suspect that he or she needs medication. Only a psychiatrist can order medication for a client, but that does not mean you have nothing to offer. Medication addresses the biological component of the illness; therapy is still needed because of the months or years of stress built up around the problems.

In a hospital or an agency setting you may get to offer counseling as part of an EAP service to another organization. You are actually doing the "same old stuff"—but with people from a specific agency or organization.

In private practice in particular, you see some fairly high-functioning clients (as compared to the chronically disturbed former mental patients that one case-manages in the community: the schizophrenics and some difficult-to-manage manic-depressives). Sometimes you have to remind yourself that you are seeing these high-functioning clients to *help* them, not make tennis dates with them. You cannot blur your boundaries when you are a social worker; friends do not counsel friends. As a professional you must remain objective, and to do that you have to isolate your relationship. (For more information on the therapist's role in treating emotionally disturbed people, read our book: *Coping with Emotional Disorders.* In it we discuss what goes on in therapy from the client's perspective.)

The private practitioner additionally has to bill clients, help them fill out insurance forms, write letters in their behalf substantiating a need for treatment, and keep treatment plans and notes accurate and up-to-date.

The clinical social worker (the therapist) not only supervises other unlicensed—or new—personnel; he or she also receives consultation on his or her cases.

The Good Points

Although very often exhausting, therapy is just as often exhilarating. You can get energized from helping a person sort out his difficulties, and you are rewarded when someone "connects" in a meaningful way with what you are saying. The progress may be miniscule at times, but the successes are still there—and they feel just as good.

Private practice is viewed by those in the field as a lucrative, rewarding way to make a living. You work with higher functioning people and you are paid $75 an hour. You hone both your clinical skills (you have to be good to survive in this field) and your business sense (since you manage your own practice). Private practice is the cream of the crop of clinical jobs.

When you have paid your dues in a psychiatric hospital—particularly if you were good at what you did—your skills are transferable to most of the other jobs. Inpatient work is demanding, varied, and important; if you can be effective in that kind of high-pressure environment you are valuable to a variety of professions. As dim a picture as I may have painted of this social work position, it is really gratifying work. You meet all kinds of people and have the opportunity to make a difference in their lives.

This work is *never* boring because the human mind is so interesting. I am always fascinated with the resiliency of the human psyche. I myself learn from helping people sort through the pain in their lives.

In most agencies you receive a stipend (so much money per year) to spend on work-related conferences or workshops. Depending on the workshop you select, you have the opportunity to create an additional paid vacation (as well as to learn with some talented clinicians).

The Disadvantages

As much as I love this work, it has some serious disadvantages. The work—a small percentage of the time—is dangerous. People who are hearing voices do not behave predictably. They may believe that you are one of the bad guys out to get them. Sometimes, especially when you hospitalize a person against his will, you incur his or her anger. It is not uncommon to get on the wrong side of a divorced spouse, especially when you are working with the other spouse. If you anticipate a potentially dangerous confrontation, you make sure to have other people near you or you alert the police.

In inpatient work the hours are usually long, the paperwork excessive, and the pace frantic. If you can stand up under pressure (and some people actually perform *better* in those circumstances), you may not find this a liability. Organized people can handle many demands on their time.

Case management is the least desirable to many clinical social workers, who aspire to be the next "world's greatest therapist." Pay your dues; you will eventually get your chance to branch out on your own, and those former mental patients need you just as much right now.

The pay for case management positions is low, and the demands on your time are disproportionately greater.

Private practice, as potentially lucrative as it can be, is also

Photo 9   Part of the clinical social worker's job is to work with people in troubled marriages.

unsteady work. Dwain has had days when five out of eight clients canceled their appointments or didn't show. That was a loss of $75 times five, or $375. When you are counting on that money it's scary when it is not forthcoming. Then, of course, you have the unpleasant task of getting payment from clients who do not intend (or are too broke) to pay you. Playing bill collector is not my idea of a clinical service . . .

Lastly, holding someone's life in your hands (or feeling as if you do) is exhausting. Worse, sometimes you fail to keep a suicidal patient alive. Losing a client is wrenching. The little failures—the clients who do not want to change or don't want to change badly enough—are one thing, but someone's death is the ultimate rejection of your help. It is hard to accept, and it hurts.

Degree Requirements

To be a case manager (sometimes called a social worker I or Associate) in a state facility, you may need only a BSW and passing a state merit exam. In the regular clinical social work positions, however, you need the MSW and state licensure with specialization in clinical practice. Insurance companies do not have to pay health benefits for the services of either unlicensed personnel or those without the MSW. Naturally, no private clinic wants to hire someone for whose services they cannot be reimbursed.

In a hospital setting you supposedly can practice without the MSW as long as you have a Master's degree. Even when I was working in just such a capacity, the rules were changing. More and more, hospitals prefer to hire MSWs who can be licensed as clinical social workers. You are well advised to get your MSW in the first place.

Opportunities in the Field

Because the more advanced degrees are now being sought, persons with only the BSW or a degree in a related field are being pushed out of these jobs, thereby creating a need for social workers with good clinical skills and the MSW. If you are willing to start in an inpatient setting, you can get a job eventually. There is always a need for dedicated clinical social workers, and the turnover in hospitals is fairly reliable.

As usual, more women are counselors because more women have the MSW. Men in this field often move into administrative roles or private practice. In Dwain's current position at a private psychiatric clinic, he is one of two male social workers among nine women. When I worked in a hospital (in its start-up phase), there were six clinicians and one male department head. Three of us were women. Since then, one of the men has gone into private practice, one branched out into EAP work at the state university, and the third moved into an administrative position. I left the field, but the two other women remain as clinicians.

Opportunities for Advancement

In this job you have plenty of chances to make more money if you have the right credentials and gain your experience first.

Clinical social workers possess the type of skills needed for a variety of other jobs, including EAP work and organizational service. Honing your skills in the lower-paying jobs enables you to transfer those skills into better-paying positions. You can move laterally into other clinical positions at agencies that pay better (perhaps because of private funding sources), or you can move upward into supervisory positions that pay more.

Managing your own private practice or acting as a consultant to organizations are other ways to increase your earnings and satisfy your longing for independence. As long as you have the advanced degree (the MSW or DSW), you can move into various other social work jobs—teaching included.

How to Break into this Job

When you have gone as far in your education as you can afford (which preferably means getting your MSW), you can take one of the appropriate state merit exams to work in a state-run facility (either a mental health center or a hospital) as a clinical social worker—probably called a Social Worker I, II, III, or higher. As in any other state job, you are placed on a register for that position, and when your name rises high enough on the list it is sent to a supervisor for an interview. You can increase your chances for getting the job or speed up the process by applying at various agencies. You may start your search with the state employment (or personnel) office where the tests are given, but you should keep checking with specific employers—without making a nuisance of yourself.

During your schooling, spend a field placement in a mental health agency. Some people have walked into jobs right after college because of their practicums and the contacts they made at those agencies.

You can work as a psychiatric aide at a hospital or mental health center while you are still in school or after you get out. The pay is minimum wage, and you are at the bottom of the totem pole, but you can't ask for better experience, and the references you can get will help immeasurably in your career pursuits.

Attend NASW meetings; stay in touch with your social work friends from graduate school. When an opening crops up in your field you want "those in the know" to think of *you*. Keep your eyes and ears open.

Helpful Hints on the Job

1. Respect the patient's and client's confidentiality. That means not chuckling about someone in the lobby where others might think you're talking about *them*.
2. Read the current literature in social work and mental health in particular. Research is always presenting new discoveries.
3. Read all the journals in your field, even if it means spending an hour or so a week in the library.
4. Behave professionally at all times.
5. *Don't get smug*. You won't be the world's greatest therapist. Once a client told me that I was the most wonderful therapist in the whole world (which I believed) and that she would forever be in my debt (which I appreciated). The very next client to walk through my door told me that

if I didn't get my act together and give her some real help
she wasn't going to come back. (That brought me back to
earth.)

6. Spend more time with your ears open and your mouth
shut. Resist the temptation to show off all the wisdom you
have stored within. No one else is interested.

7. See the good in your clients—because they probably have
no concept of it. Your positive regard for them may be all
they are aware of in the beginning. Help them find their
strengths.

Chapter XIII

Other Social Work Opportunities

This chapter discusses a variety of other social work positions. Some are quite unusual, and the salary ranges are highly variable.

One of my friends had been a medical social worker for thirteen years. Saying she felt "unchallenged," she quit her job last spring and joined the Peace Corps as a social worker. She has been assigned to a small village in West Africa now that her two to three months of training are over. Georgia Ann had to learn a new language and adjust to a culture quite unlike anything she has ever experienced. She wrote me, "The sights, sounds, and smells in combination with each other are beyond my imagination."

What will she be doing in her community site? "My village asked for a village developer to assist mobilizing human resources to build a clinic, latrines, wells, co-ops, and assess for other appropriate industries."

As a social worker in the Peace Corps, Georgia Ann earns only a monthly living allotment that won't set her apart from the villagers and then a lump sum at the end of service. Her house has no electricity or running water. But she is learning firsthand about a different culture and has the opportunity to make a lasting impression on the people. Social workers are, as a rule, good organizers and as such are effective workers for the Peace Corps. You organize people to build, come together, and improve their basic conditions such as sanitation and shelter. The work is both gratifying and backbreaking. It takes incredible courage, patience, and self-sufficiency to take on these jobs. You are away from home for at least two years, having few comforts in your new surroundings, and possibly fighting off strange diseases.

If you are interested in this kind of work, you do not need an MSW, nor do you even need to be a social worker. All you need do is contact the Peace Corps branch in your community and request information. Or you can call 1-800-424-8580, or write to The Peace Corps, 1990 "K" Street, NW, Washington, DC 20526.

It might be useful to get your degree first, however; then you'll have it to fall back on when you have finished your Peace Corps stint. The minimum age is 21 years; there is no upper age limit. Of those in my friend's training class some were women in their 70s.

You may be interested in hospice work, which is a combination of a clinical and medical social worker. A hospice is a homelike setting for persons who are terminally ill. People go there to die, rather than in a hospital stuck full of IVs and left to deal with changing shifts of nurses and the impersonality of the medical environment.

Your job, then, as a social worker is to help the patient and his family accept his approaching death. You do this by listening to them all and by helping them to say their good-byes so that no one is left with regrets. Of course, it means being able to deal with death yourself. We all accept on an impersonal level that people die; it is far harder to *watch* someone die— someone to whom you have grown attached, someone who may seem too young and vital to die. If you can handle your tasks with sensitivity and equanimity, you will be a boon to this profession. There is great demand for social workers with the training (and more significant, the disposition) to work in this setting, particularly with the threat of AIDS increasing.

If you are interested in this work, spend your practicum

(in apprenticeship with another social worker) in a hospice. Although your abilities and sensitivity are of more practical use, you would be wise to get your MSW degree. Read all the books you can by Elisabeth Kubler-Ross, who is renowned for her work with the terminally ill. Deal with your own "death anxiety" first, so that you can bring compassion—not fear—to the job.

Some social workers work at the Travelers Aid Society. Originally these workers assisted staff in hospitals and welfare offices to finance transients on their way home. For that reason they often worked in bus or train stations or at airports. Because of the shift in attention to the homeless population, social workers in this agency now focus 75% of their work on resettling the homeless. Most of their work is crisis-oriented and involves making referrals to other service agencies. Sometimes the Travelers Aid social worker uncovers abuse in the families she serves; although the abuse is reported, the social worker still works with the families to strengthen appropriate ties.

Like the clinical social worker (but on a lesser scale), this social worker counsels some street people who remain in her community and still need resources and support to manage their lives. She is not unlike the medical and Human Services social workers who continually link these people to other community funds. It is her job to help them find food and shelter and to provide funds to go back "home" if they have one. The job is at the low end of the pay scale because it is an entry-level job, despite the sophisticated skills required. Because it is privately funded through donations and the United Way, it cannot afford to offer real pay incentives.

Travelers Aid work can be used as a stepping-stone to other jobs because the skills you cultivate are easily transferable. The MSW is not required at this time.

Other social workers who may practice the same skills as the clinical social worker work in specialized fields: in substance-abuse or eating-disorder programs. They may be recovering themselves, but they nonetheless possess the educational background and experience to counsel people in these programs. Substance-abuse programs have their own special focus. Some advocate the use of antidepressants to treat the patient's underlying depression once the alcohol and drugs are removed. Other programs believe that reliance on drugs is part of the problem.

In eating-disorder groups the social worker not only must possess good clinical skills but also be well versed in the subterfuges of eating-disordered clients. The anorexic or bulimic client dreads "getting fat" and fears giving control over her eating patterns to the therapist. Working with resistant clients is exhausting work. The gains are few; the losses are substantial.

If you are interested in working in these specialized programs—and for some people it is personally rewarding, challenging work—I suggest you hire on first as an aide while you are still in school. You need the MSW degree, but the practical experience of working closely with clients on a day-to-day basis is invaluable.

The pay varies in this work, as do the specific tasks. If a program is privately funded, you stand to earn more money. Sometimes you can work in a clinical capacity, establishing your credentials so that you can then hire out as a consultant. As a consultant you can name your own salary.

In most of the jobs mentioned in this chapter, you must possess the ability to work with low-income people. It is not enough to "want to help them"; as traditional social workers find in working in low-income neighborhoods, those who need help resent being in that position. You must understand that people in less fortunate circumstances are not less human. And you, as the helper, are not *more* human.

When you work with people in different cultures, do not attempt to suffocate them with your culture. Our ways are not necessarily better, nor are they even helpful to some people. Respect other people's ways of life; don't impose your own on them. When you work with people who seem to lack control over their impulses, impose some restraint, if necessary, but don't get smug. We all have our problems; we're never immune.

Photo 10 These teens are working for "Teen Line" a hotline that answers questions on all subjects for teenagers.

Chapter XIV

Learning in Your First Job

In this last chapter I'm going to take you through your first few weeks on a job. No matter that it isn't your dream job; it is important to learn how to behave on any job because you won't earn good references for your next job if you mess up on the first.

You don't have to be an inexperienced teenager not to know how to behave on the job. I was in my mid-twenties and working as a social worker when I got clued in to some of my own misbehavior on the job. Back then, when work was slow or clients didn't keep appointments I often had a block of free time. Most of the other social workers had similar free time, but whereas they chose to spend theirs in their offices (with the doors closed), I sat with the receptionist, comparing notes on our weekends. Since I wasn't talking loudly, and I wasn't discussing clients' cases, I thought this behavior was acceptable. One day, a supervisor took me aside. She told me that although I behaved professionally in all other respects, this sitting in the lobby was hurting my image.

"How's that?" I asked. "I see my clients. I'm caught up on my paperwork, and I'm not talking about anyone."

"I'll tell you how it looks to other people," she said. "It looks as if you have nothing else to do so you sit out here gossiping."

"But I've done all my work," I objected.

"They don't know that," she said. "What matters is how it

looks. If you have nothing better to do with your time, read the professional journals. Volunteer to cover an admission or two, but either stay busy or stay out of sight."

Looking back on that incident now, I hate to think I needed someone to tell me that. So, to spare you some of the embarrassment I went through, let me share some thoughts on handling that first job or two. If I am now an expert, it's only because I've made so many of these mistakes.

On any job, you should spend more of your time listening than talking. You cannot figure out what your tasks are if you're trying to second-guess your boss. Let her talk. It's discourteous to interrupt, anyway.

Don't bring personal effects to the office. If you have a temporary job you only create a mess, and even in a private office you don't want to create the impression that you live there. Save the pictures of your boyfriend, girlfriend, or spouse for your bedroom. Clients don't need to know where your love interests lie.

If you choose to decorate your work space, use taste and good sense. Bringing in expensive knickknacks will only distract you from your job. If you spend time worrying about art objects on your desk, pack them up and take them home.

No matter how professional you are otherwise, don't make yourself visible in unproductive ways. Customers and clients don't like to discover that an employee is bored in his job or looks it. Leave your books at home if you can't keep your hands off them during work time. Also don't lounge around the reception area looking as if you're gossiping (even if you're not). You'll only invite criticism.

If you have some free time, catch up on your paperwork. If you are caught up, take advantage of the break by volunteering to help somewhere else.

When you first start working—no matter where—be careful of the alliances you make. Every office has factions, and in the beginning you won't know who belongs to which faction— who hates whom. It is best to be friendly with everyone but wary of entanglements. Making buddies (or worse, lovers) of

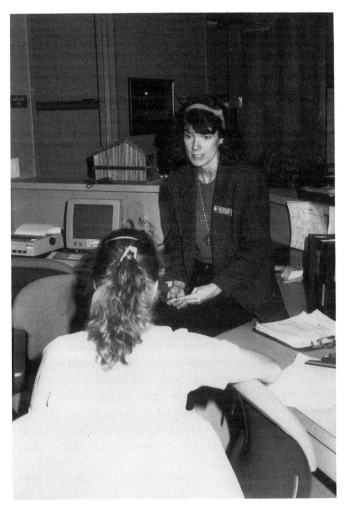

Photo 11   Don't sit around on desks in your spare time. Stay productive.

your colleagues is asking for trouble. Try to keep your work separate from your personal life.

Speaking of your personal life, it has no place in the office. If you are too upset to work, either take the day off or explain to your boss—and only your boss—why you can't perform. No one needs to learn that your father has lost his job, that you just broke off with your fiancée. If you are working with clients you are there to focus on *their* problems, not your own. Take care of your personal stuff on your own time.

Don't gossip—*ever*. It is unprofessional, and it reflects worse on you than on the one gossiped about.

If you have to hand in reports, be sure your writing is legible. People who have to type your reports and other social workers who have to rely on your written notes will be frustrated if they can't read them. In hospitals where documentation is essential for accreditation, administrators expect you to keep accurate and legible records. If you don't, they lose money and you are likely to be out of a job.

Wear appropriate clothing to your job. Don't dress either provocatively for your collegues or shabbily for your low-income clients. Being careless of your appearance is discourteous to others who have to be in your company.

Do I need to remind you to show up *on time* and in condition to work? Sporting a hangover, a two-day beard, or the clothes you wore the day before is no way to impress your supervisors.

Smoking rules are posted in most agencies. Respect the rules. In many facilities (particularly health settings) smoking is not allowed on the premises. Sneaking smokes in the bathroom is not just frowned on; it is not tolerated.

Although chewing gum is not quite the equivalent of chewing tobacco, it is still unattractive to watch and obnoxious to hear. Chew gum when you are not in contact with the public (and that includes colleagues).

Let's talk about "leave time." Most of you will receive a certain number of hours a month for sick leave or vacation time. Use your time wisely. Earning a sick day a month and using it as fast as you accrue it will only antagonize people, who will think you are just playing sick. And don't call in sick to go shopping at the mall. Chances are someone will see you there. Murphy's Law decrees that "whatever can go wrong *will* go wrong," so be aware that little lies can backfire. If you want to impress people with your dependability, then for Pete's sake be dependable!

When you are fresh out of college you are typically full of ideas to "change the world." Those of us who have been tarnished by years in the profession can use your idealism and enthusiasm. But problems crop up if you butt heads with your colleagues (or supervisors) over all of your ideas. Often there are reasons why the old ways work better. Watch for a while to learn the ways. Offer suggestions when you have had time to see how things work at your agency. Don't embarrass your supervisor (or anyone else, for that matter) in a meeting where others will witness the verbal clash. Express your concerns privately to the person with whom you are in conflict. Don't go over a supervisor's head immediately; that strategy backfires more often than it works. Don't create the impression that you are difficult to work with; such comments become part of your "invisible file" at an agency. I said in an earlier chapter that there are times to take a stand and times to stand back. Learn to tell the difference.

Sometimes you will face conflicts of conscience. When Dwain was working as an aide in a nursing home years ago, he discovered that the private patients received preferential care over the welfare recipients. Even the food the two groups received was different. At the time the home ws being investigated for those very practices. One of the investigators wanted to talk to Dwain about it. Should Dwain have admitted the preferential treatment, which would surely have meant losing his job? Should he have kept quiet and continued to work at a place that practiced such inequities? Or should he have kept quiet and tried himself to make up for the differences in treatment?

In such a predicament you have to weigh the pros and cons and decide whether your conscience will permit you to stay. If the pay is good or the economic times are bad you won't want to lose your job. In that case, don't bad-mouth your supervisors to salvage your conscience. If you work in an agency, support it, and that means not talking ill of any of its employees. If you are looking for another job, the worst thing you can do is bad-mouth your previous employer in an interview. The new agency will wonder what kind of personality conflict you got into and when you will get into similar difficulties again.

Lastly, don't take on more extracurricular activities than you can handle. It's all well and good to want to "fit in" quickly, but volunteering (and thus, overextending yourself) to host every party or cover every news event will wear you out. Take on only those tasks for which you have time. Set priorities so that you end up doing the important things or the things for which you have talent. And sometimes don't volunteer at all.

When we start out in the world of work we all make mistakes. Some of those mistakes we can laugh about later. Oddly enough, people never seem to learn from doing something *right*. They learn best from mistakes.

If you blow it on the job a few times, don't despair. As long as you learn from the experience, consider it a lesson in growing up. Fortunately, we never have to provide a history of our mistakes to people. We just live and learn, as the saying goes. And some learn more quickly than others . . .

Bibliography

Compton, Beulah, and Galaway, Burt. *Social Work Processes.*
Illinois: The Dorsey Press, 1989.

Germain, Carel, and Gitterman, Alex. *The Life Model of Social Work Practice.* New York: Columbia University Press, 1980.

Judson, Clara Ingram. *City Neighbor. The Story of Jane Addams.* New York: Charles Scribner's Sons, 1951.

McNeer, May, and Ward, Lynd. *Armed with Courage.* New York: Abington Press, 1957.

Peavy, Linda, and Smith, Ursula. *Dreams into Deeds.* New York: Charles Scribner's Sons, 1985.

Index